11 CARDINAL RULES FOR A SUCCESSFUL JOB INTERVIEW

- Never arrive late to the interview
- Be mindful of the physical appearance you project
- Unfreeze your face—smile
- Shake hands firmly
- Present a positive attitude
- Listen attentively
- Show enthusiasm
- Show that you are mindful of the company and its operation
- Don't talk too much and talk yourself out of a job
- Approach the question of salary cautiously
- Get the interviewer to like you

KNOW WHAT TO EXPECT IN A JOB INTERVIEW! IT'S THE CONFIDENCE-BUILDER THAT MAKES A DIFFERENCE!

From the moment a face-to-face meeting begins, everything about you—your appearance, speech, ability, personality, even your smile—is being assessed. It's up to you to create a favorable impression. And preparation is the only sure-fire way to make an important job interview a winning experience.

Now, here in this superb updated edition, you'll find the proven advice, strategies and techniques necessary to skillfully handle an interview—and achieve successful results. Start today! Learn how to:

- Dress appropriately for your interview
- Prepare an attention-getting resume
- Increase your poise—and reduce tension
- Use proper grammar at all times
- Answer questions with ease—and ask the "right" ones
- Avoid the pitfalls of job interviews—all 63 of them
- Apply the "11 Cardinal Rules for a Successful Interview"

ABOUT THE AUTHOR:

J. I. Biegeleisen has been a nationally known writer and career coordinator for more than 20 years. He has served as Supervisor and Assistant Principal at a leading New York City high school where he also acted as liaison between school, trade unions and employment agencies. He has frequently served on the interview committee with the Board of Examiners in the screening and selection of candidates for teaching positions in the New York City school system. Currently, Mr. Biegeleisen is engaged in job counseling and is a frequent lecturer on career guidance and job procurement techniques. His advice column, "The Job Market and You," appears weekly in both the *Fort Lauderdale News* and the *Sun-Sentinel*, with a combined readership of over 650,000.

MAKE YOUR
JOB INTERVIEW
A SUCCESS

MAKE YOUR
JOB INTERVIEW
A SUCCESS

A Guide for the Career-Minded Job Seeker

J.I. BIEGELEISEN

AN ARCO BOOK
DISTRIBUTED BY PRENTICE HALL TRADE
NEW YORK

An Arco Book
Distributed by Prentice Hall Trade
A Division of Simon & Schuster, Inc.
Gulf + Western Building
One Gulf + Western Plaza
New York, New York 10023

PRENTICE HALL TRADE is a trademark of Simon & Schuster, Inc.

Manufactured in the United States of America

1 2 3 4 5 6 7 8 9 10

Library of Congress Cataloging-in-Publication Data

Biegeleisen, J. I. (Jacob Israel), 1910–
   Make your job interview a success.

   Includes index.
   1. Employment interviewing. I. Title.
HF5549.5.I6B5   1987   650.1′4   87-19294
ISBN 0-13-545716-5

We should all be concerned about the future because we will have to spend the rest of our lives there.

Charles Franklin Kettering

CONTENTS

MAKE YOUR
JOB INTERVIEW
A SUCCESS

1

BY WAY OF INTRODUCTION

Hello!

In your ongoing search for reading material to help prepare you for a job interview, you surely have come across a number of other books on interview techniques. There are dozens of them around. The trouble is that very few of them are directed to you—the job applicant. Written by high-powered professional interviewers, such books are primarily meant to serve as technical guides for their colleagues in the field. This doesn't mean you can't glean valuable insights on the criteria by which a professional interviewer assesses a job applicant. You definitely can. Nonetheless, you somehow get the feeling that you've picked up the wrong book and that its author is, in a manner of speaking, more of an adversary than a friend. He is apprising his fellow interviewers on the diverse means of sizing up a candidate for the job on hand, even if it means deliberately tripping him up along the way, if need be, to get below the surface.

Make Your Job Interview a Success—the book you hold in your hand now,— is written by someone on your side of the interview table and is intended specifically for you—the career-minded job candidate.

Though the main thrust of this book is on interview procedures, you'll find in it, I am sure, abundant material to guide you through the many preliminary steps leading to an interview and culminating in a job offer: resume preparation; contacting prospective employers directly or through other means; how to make an impressive appearance; questions the interviewer is likely to ask you, and those you can ask him.

Featured in this book are 11 never-fail cardinal rules, which, if correctly applied, guarantee you a successful outcome in any job interview that you may be preparing for—now, tomorrow, or the days ahead.

A special section is devoted to questions and answers covering the various aspects of job procurement and interview situations, among which there undoubtedly will be many that concern you personally and reflect your needs and interests.

Throughout the book, for reasons of simplification and to avoid resorting to indirect phrasing or other artful grammatical circumlocutions, I have used the masculine pronoun *he* (and its extensions—his, him), although the intended meaning in most cases applies to both sexes. Contemporary writers of how-to books continually wrestle with this problem and for the most part make use of the same literary expediency.

It is my sincere hope that you'll find within these pages the down-to-earth counseling you have long been looking for in book form, and that you will think of the author not merely as a professional career consultant, but as a personal friend as well.

J. I. Biegeleisen

AN OVERVIEW OF TRADITIONAL JOB-SEARCH TECHNIQUES

WHAT DO YOU think constitutes an effective job-search campaign, and in your opinion what are the stepping stones leading to a job interview?

Going through the routine of registering with an employment agency or job counseling service? No. Answering an ad? No. Placing an ad? No. Keep sending out more and more resumes? No. Making "cold turkey" calls and ringing doorbells? No. Letting relatives, friends, and friends of friends know that you are job hunting? No. And if you've been bumped from a plum job that you thought was secure from here to eternity, thumbing through a copy of *When Bad Things Happen to Good People*? Again, no. And as a last resort, praying for Lady Luck not to pass you by? You can't bank on any of these individually. However, put them together as a well-coordinated, multi-faceted approach to job procurement—and you can't miss! A combination of fine-tuned planning and tireless persistence, plus a good measure of faith and confidence, are bound to pay off in invitations to interviews and the kind of attractive job offers you're looking for.

Let's take a closer view of some of the more tangible pathways open to the enterprising job seeker.

HELP WANTED ADS

The reason so many job seekers turn first to help wanted ads is that this medium offers a direct line of communication between job seeker and advertiser.

You may have been told by some cynical job seekers (of whom there is no shortage), and even by some professional counselors, that publicly advertised job openings are not worth following up—that most ads don't present the facts as they really are, and blind ads in particular are not infrequently outright fakes. Categorically, this is just not true. The fact is, it is through advertised job openings that hundreds of thousands of people every year find their niche in the labor market, not only for routine low-paying jobs (as is commonly believed) but for career positions in the $40,000-a-year-and-up salary level.

Types of Help Wanted Ads

Help wanted ads fall into three general categories:

An "open" ad placed by the employer. In this type of ad, the employer may identify himself by firm name, address, and/or phone number. Since his identity is known, the job applicant has the choice of contacting him by phone, by mail, or by dropping in to see him in person.

A "blind" or box number ad placed by the employer. Here the employer, for reasons of his own, chooses to mask his identity. The only way he can be reached is by mail addressed to a coded number shown in the ad. Incidentally, as a job seeker, you have the same privilege of placing a blind ad of your own in the Situation Wanted column should you wish to defer revealing who you are until you have established contact with a likely employer.

An ad placed by an employment agency. Here the point of contact is the employment agency, not the employer directly. Although the nature of the position is spelled out, the applicant doesn't know who the would-be employer is until he has registered with the agency and an interview is arranged for him.

Analyzing a Help Wanted Ad

The typical help wanted ad is most often composed of two parts: (a) what the employer looks for—experience, skills, personal attributes, etc. and (b) what the employer offers—salary, fringe benefits, opportunities for advancement, location, etc.

Here is how this shapes up in the following example.

> SECRETARY-RECEPTIONIST—Experienced, well-groomed, pleasing personalitiy, knowledge of word processing, typing, to work for two young account executives. Beautiful, modern midtown offices, $250 weekly to start.

Part "a" of the ad calls for an experienced applicant with certain attributes and skills. This is what the employer wants, but notice that the wording here adroitly

VARIED PATHWAYS
TO JOB INTERVIEWS

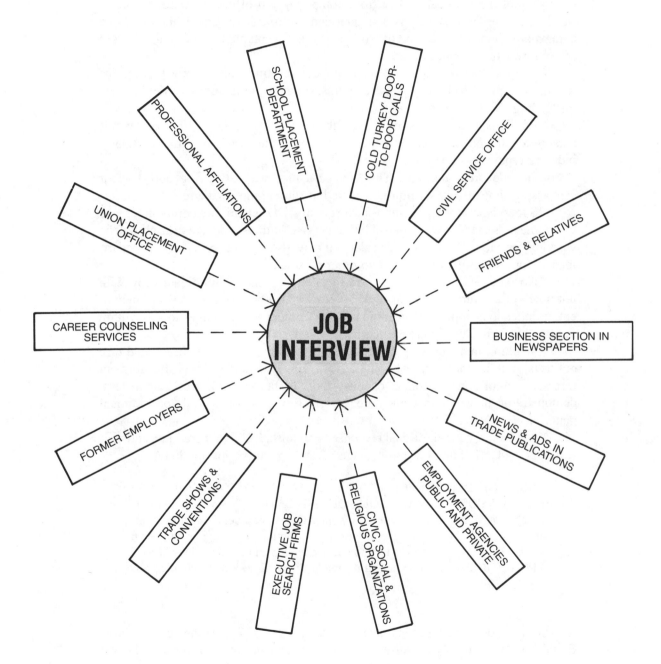

leads into part ''b,'' which is phrased to look especially inviting to the applicant. Here the employer makes it a point to mention pleasant office surroundings, ideal location, and the prospect of working with two account executives. Though the salary mentioned (somewhat below the going rate) is listed last, the phrase ''to start'' infers that increases are in order.

In times of economic prosperity, it is the job seeker who is in the driver's seat. Part ''a'.' of an ad is much less demanding, while part ''b'' is made inviting to tempt the applicant away from competing job offers. In times of recession, when the labor supply is abundant and job openings scarce, the employer is far more choosy in the type of worker who is acceptable to him, and therefore offers fewer lures or promises.

It's up to the job seeker to read between the lines and carefully study the wording of an ad to be cognizant of phrases that are ambiguous or deliberately misleading. Watch out for these:

''Earnings up to'': This could mean there is no fixed salary. What you earn is what you make on commissions. It may also entail piecework or some ''cottage'' industry type of occupation.

''Outside order taking'': This can be a nice way of saying door-to-door canvassing, not merely writing up orders but scrounging for them.

''Supervisory position for those who qualify'': Often this is a come-on for jobs where the person hired will ostensibly ''supervise'' others who like himself will be working for a lower-than-average salary. It may also mean supervising a ''department'' consisting of just one or two other persons.

''No experience required'': A sure sign that the salary is inordinately low with not much of a future to look forward to. It may also be a bogus ad with intent to entrap ingenuous applicants in some scheme or other that manages to stay within the law but is of questionable integrity.

''Working in advertising promotion'': This high sounding phrase could turn out to be nothing more than slipping advertising flyers under doors, handing out free samples of a new product on busy thoroughfares, serving as a short-term demonstrator in a department store, or stuffing envelopes with promotional material.

What would your emotional response be to this ad, shown here in its entirety, which is evidently aimed at the managerial and executive job market?

TIRED OF BEING SECOND IN COMMAND TO SOMEONE WHO DOESN'T POSSESS HALF YOUR QUALIFICATIONS? An opening exists for aggressive and innovative man or woman to head new department in an up-and-coming food processing firm. A once-in-a-lifetime career opportunity with top money prospects. Could lead to part ownership and earnings in excess of $150,000 a year. Send letter and resume to P. O. Box 568, Rockville, MD 20651.

Sounds good? Yes, but is it a legitimate job offer? What is the actual salary? Could it possibly involve a substantial cash investment not mentioned in the ad? These and similar doubts can be cleared up by contacting the advertiser. There's nothing to be lost but the cost of a postage stamp.

SITUATION WANTED ADS

If you were to ask a group of employment counselors, "Can you expect any results by placing an ad in the Situation Wanted column of the classified section?", you'd get conflicting opinions. Some would unequivocally say, "By all means." Others would give you an outright, "No." Most would hedge and say "It all depends————", in the thought that it's the safest answer to give because so many factors play a part in determining the value of a Situation Wanted ad—where the ad appears, what day of the week, the phrasing of the ad, your particular qualifications, the competition in the field, the current economic situation. All work for or against your chances of getting an invitation to meet your would-be employer face-to-face.

This much is certain. When you place a Situation Wanted ad, you have an inherent advantage in your favor. It is *you* who will be the one to receive and be able to screen offers and have the option to select those that look most promising. The question of how many, or the kind of replies you get, takes us right back to those variable factors of where and when you advertise, what you have to offer, and how the ad is worded—plus a dose of good luck. Among the replies there will no doubt be some that are anxious to have you sign up for an expensive course on how to get a job with a future, client-hungry employment agencies on the lookout for prospects, or firms that have no actual job openings but want to test the labor market. Your own good sense will help you separate the wheat from the chaff. All in all, you'll have opened up another path to explore new opportunities, hopefully leading to a job interview. Many enterprising job seekers have found that an ad placed in the Situation Wanted column pays off. If it works for them, it may work for you, too.

Phrasing a Situation Wanted Ad

The best approach is to state at the very outset just what kind of position you're looking for, what's special or unique about your qualifications, and factual evidence of your ability. Practical considerations should prompt you to say this in a minimum number of words, bearing in mind that the more words, the higher the cost. Rewrite the words of your ad as many times as necessary, trimming it here and there to make each word count. Then give the final version this test: Does the ad show your as-yet-unknown employer how you can be an asset to his company, or what he stands to gain by employing you?

Let's analyze the Situation Wanted ad shown here to see how well this job seeker succeeds in anticipating the needs of the employer.

ADV. MGR. WHO SELLS—Triple your adv. $ returns with my 3-way ad plan. 12 yrs creative adm. exp. Acct. exec, copywriter, art dir., heavy on dealer-distrib. promo, direct mail, trade show agny liaison, dealer programs. Nat'l coop advg campaign. V 428 Times.

The job seeker here is in the advertising profession and the fast-paced phrasing of the ad is evidence of his specialized talents. He starts off with the pronouncement that he is an advertising manager who sells. And what is the first thing he mentions? Something that he wants? No. He immediately zeroes in on what he knows will catch the employer's eye, "Triple your advertising dollar returns ————." He then goes on to say that he can bring this about by means of a unique "3-way ad plan" he has originated. And he is no "Johnny-come-lately" with untried ideas! He has had 12 years of creative merchandising and administrative experience to show for it. Moreover, this experience extends over many diversified areas—all of which are related. The entire ad, including the catchy headline, is condensed into 41 well-chosen words which take no more than 1¼ inches of space in print.

By way of contrast, here is an ad placed by someone looking for a position as Executive Secretary and Administrative Assistant.

> EXEC. SECY.—ADMIN ASST—Exceptional, perceptive, dependable, expeditious, personable. Superior skills, diversified background (including legal). Willing to consider $350 weekly starting salary. T3214 Times

The applicant claims to be exceptional, perceptive, etc., etc.; however, these are hardly more than self-serving generalities.

Here is a revised version of this ad. It's interesting to see that claims are backed up with facts. Mention is made of specific skills, length of experience, and a reference to educational background.

> EXEC. SECY., RIGHT ARM TO BUSY ADMINISTRATOR—Degree. 8 yrs. diversified exp. (corporate, p.r., legal). Do own correspondence, typing 80 w.p.m. Happy to start at $350. T 3214 Times.

Which of the two applicants would you want to interview if you needed a capable Executive Secretary/Administrative Assistant? The answer is obvious.

EMPLOYMENT AGENCIES

It's been estimated that employment agencies, all told, succeed in placing no more than 20% of employable people out of work or those wishing to switch jobs. In terms of percentages, 20% may not seem much, but it amounts to millions of job seekers placed each year. The remaining 80% find jobs through their own efforts and initiative.

Although employment agencies have been frequently criticized and often called onto the carpet for ineptness and, in some instances, malfeasance, they nevertheless render a valuable service to employers and job seekers alike. Employers use them to reach qualified workers; job seekers use them to locate would-be employers. To best appreciate the role played by an employment agency, think of the counselor who handles your case as a mutual friend of both you and the employer—someone trying to arrange a blind date between the two of you.

Private Employment Agencies

These agencies operate on a fee-paid basis—a fee either paid by the employer or the applicant, depending upon the fluctuating supply and demand of the labor market. When there is a shortage of labor unilaterally or in a specific area of work, the employer eager to get qualified people will pay the agency fee. Conversely, in a period of economic recession, the applicant may be willing to assume the fee in its entirety, or share it with the prospective employer.

Nationwide there are approximately 7500 licensed, private employment agencies; New York City alone has between 600 to 700 of them. The actual number varies at any one time because of the high rate of turnover. New ones come into the field practically overnight; others close up and leave.

In large metropolitan areas, agencies are apt to specialize, concentrating either in one or in a cluster of related occupational fields. For example, there are agencies known for computer and data processing positions; others make a speciality of accounting, finance, hospital and nursing jobs, sales and marketing research, engineering, secretarial and office positions, and a variety of blue-collar occupations. It makes sense to select an agency that has established a good reputation in job procurement in your particular line of work. Agencies located in smaller communities are more often set up to handle jobs in diversified areas of employment.

For an extended listing of employment agencies and their respective occupational specialities, look in the Yellow Pages of your phone book. Better still, refer to their ads in the classified or display section of your newspapers and trade journals.

State Employment Service (SES)

In the dark days of the Great Depression, the Federal Government established a free employment service, the prime purpose of which was to find jobs for the unprecedented number of unemployed people who could not afford private employment agencies. This service has for many years now been handled by the individual states. Currently there are approximately 1700 SES offices throughout the country.

While primarily set up for job-placement contacts, the SES does counseling and testing and makes referrals for those who need to upgrade their skills for gainful employment. Due consideration is given to young people just entering the field of work, retirees wishing to return to the workforce on a part- or full-time basis, minority groups with language and/or skill deficiencies, as well as the handicapped.

There is never a charge for guidance or job placement. Counselors are friendly and helpful.

School Placement Offices

Today nearly all schools and colleges provide job placement and counseling services for their students. The placement counselor acting as liaison between school and industry keeps abreast of the current job market in relation to the specialized subject areas in the curriculum. Students are free to consult the counselor on job opportunities as well as for referrals to specific job openings.

The door of the school placement office is always open for anyone regardless of when he graduated. A school's concern for its students does not end with the graduation exercises.

Trade-Union Placement Offices

The typical trade-union placement office is similar in operation to the SES in that it charges no fee for job placement. However, unlike the SES, the union limits placement privileges to its membership only and has direct contact with employers.

If you hold a union card and are out of work, your local is the first port-of-call to line up a job for you. Indeed, one of the functions of any labor organization is to act as a clearing house for job placement. Union jobs are hardly ever publicly advertised—and that's to your advantage, if you happen to be a bona fide member of the trade union in your occupation.

Company-operated Employment Offices

Most larger companies with a sizeable number of employees run their own in-house employment office as part of the Personnel Department to serve the employment needs of the company exclusively.

Corridor rumors have it that if you're looking for an important job, bypass the Personnel Department. Make your availability known to the division head, district manager, or anyone else with hiring authority. Don't waste your time with the monkey when you can talk directly to the organ grinder. The view is held that the Personnel Department not infrequently is run by a roster of functionaries who are not much more above the rank of clerk and who have little decision-making authority. Be that as it may, unless you have someone pulling for you in the front office, the normal channel for job placement in any large business establishment is the Personnel Department.

Placement by Quasi-public, Religious, and Fraternal Organizations

The Urban League, B'nai B'rith, the "Y," and similar organizations often provide career guidance and job referrals as a public service, either without cost or on payment of a nominal fee. So do many religious and fraternal groups. In extended job-search planning, these sources should by no means be ignored.

"Temp" Employment Agencies

Agencies specializing in temp employment are in the business of supplying personnel to individual firms on a stipulated "cost-plus" basis. The temp worker pays no fee to the agency.

When signing up with a temp you are, in a manner of speaking, rented out on an hourly, per diem, or weekly basis. Your real employer, that is, the one who pays your salary, is the agency, not the company you happen to be working for at the time.

Working as a temp has a built-in feature which attracts those who are not able to or do not wish to tie themselves down to a fixed-time schedule. Included in this category are those with young children or other dependents to take care of, seasonal actors, people attending school either one part of the day or another, retirees who wish to retain their sense of usefulness through gainful employment and as a practical means to supplement their social security income, as well as those adventurous spirits who seek a variety in work experience.

Employers look with favor upon temp help, and for good reasons. They are released from many of the bookkeeping chores associated with maintaining a staff of regular employees. They are also absolved from the responsibilities of paying the traditional fringe benefits that full-time employees have long been accustomed to—vacations and holidays, sick leave, pensions, health insurance, and all the rest of it.

One out of every five American workers today is employed on a part-time basis—many as temps. Among the originators of the temp employment concept are Kelly Services and Manpower Inc. There are hundreds of others in the field now, most of whom specialize in a select group of trades and occupations.

Executive Search Firms

Indelicately referred to as "flesh peddlers," "head hunters," or "body snatchers," executive search firms act as talent scouts for companies in need of individuals who it is hoped will spark lagging production, boost profits, or in some way through association help enhance the prestige of the company. It is not rare for new positions to be specifically created to fit well-known personalities into the organization.

The prime quarries of executive search firms are companies known to have outstanding, success-rated individuals on their staff. The object is to unhitch these super achievers from their present moorings to tie them up with another company offering "golden persuaders"—a more attractive money package in terms of a hefty salary increase, front-end bonuses, tempting stock options, and a cornucopia of other benefits and perks.

Executive search firms are compensated for their services by the company who commissions them, not by the recruited employee. They work mostly on a retainer plus a stipulated percentage of the recruit's first year's salary.

Currently, there are approximately 1500 to 2000 executive search firms in the United States, a rather loosely estimated figure since it includes many employment agencies who advertise themselves as recruiting firms, which they are not. Bona fide executive recruiting firms concentrate mainly on men and women in the $50,000-a-year-and-up salary bracket. It may take some time before a potential recruit is discovered and placed, but like the legendary Royal Canadian Mounties, they always get their man (or woman).

The normal course is for the recruiting firm to contact a prospect, not the other way around. Recruiting firms receive bushels of unsolicited letters of application and resumes. As someone coming in out of the cold, you have only a remote chance of being given serious consideration, and if footloose and out of work at the time, your chances are even slimmer. But though the odds are obviously stacked against you, you can never tell. If they don't seek you out, it's your prerogative to take the initiative. As the saying goes, "If the mountain doesn't come to Mohammed, then Mohammed can come to the mountain."

It's flattering if an executive recruiter approaches you. It signifies that you have reached stardom level.

CORPORATE OUTPLACEMENT FIRMS

Corporate outplacement firms are retained by large corporations to assist their displaced employees (or those about to be phased out) to get back on their feet in gainful employment elsewhere or wherever possible within the organization itself in another job category. The corporation sponsoring this type of counseling service underwrites part or all of the costs involved. In some instances, as in the case of key executives, it may come up to $15,000.

Introduced in the early 1970's, this paternalistically motivated program represents an innovative concept in labor-management relations in the United States. Since its inception, it has proven itself to be a significant morale booster for expatriated employees as well as the entire work staff, from those in the lowly shipping department to the brass in the executive penthouse.

A corporate-sponsored outplacement program bespeaks of an ongoing interest and concern on the part of the company for its employees. It pays off handsomely in heightened loyalty and the status the company holds among its peers in the industry. All in all, it makes the workforce (past and present) feel good about the company; it makes the company feel good about itself.

Outplacement firms provide group as well as individual counseling, and where necessary suggest retraining referrals for those wishing to explore career opportunities in other fields—everything short of actual placement. And no less important, they provide those who've lost their jobs through no fault of their own with the psychological support designed to mend bruised egos and regenerate self-confidence.

A growing number of major corporations are sponsoring outplacement programs of one kind or another with gratifying results. Records show that 75% of the participants are successful in finding employment in a comparatively short time, and not infrequently on a higher salary level.

It should be noted that not all outplacement programs are corporate sponsored. There are private employment agencies who call themselves "corporate outplacement firms" to attract unwary clients by this subterfuge. Experience has shown that they are not nearly as effective as outplacement firms sponsored and carefully monitored by corporations, and of course, they charge a fee.

JOB COUNSELING FIRMS

There are many varieties of job counseling firms, differing not so much in function as in the names they choose to go by and in degree of professional integrity. Some call themselves employment counselors, others occupational advisors, career management consultants, or executive counseling firms. In most states it is considered unlawful for counseling service organizations (regardless of the name they adopt) to do job placement. Counseling firms are strictly limited to function in an advisory capacity—that is all—and not to operate in direct competition with regular employment agencies. Not long ago two of New York's top career counseling firms were the subjects of an undercover investigation by the Department of Consumer Affairs for willfully conveying the impression that they place their clients as part of the service. One of the firms, when found guilty, packed up and went out of business shortly thereafter.

At the present writing only a limited number of states issue licenses to those with the proper credentials to practice professional job counseling. Elsewhere it's anybody's privilege to hang out a shingle and set himself up as counselor or job consultant. This means that the job seeker in need of guidance must establish for himself who among the many in the field are truly qualified and worth the fee asked for. Caveat emptor!

As a group, job counseling firms have a low credibility rating. There are some good ones among them but you have to search them out. This is not an easy task.

A well-established counseling firm known to have an enviable reputation can prove to be of great help to the distraught job seeker unable to fend for himself. Such an organization will include in its extensive program psychological and aptitude tests, practice interviews, resume development, salary negotiation strategy, and innovative job-search techniques—in short, everything to prepare the client with the know-how and sharpened skills to get a job on his own.

Ten Tips On Selecting and Evaluating Job Counseling Firms

1. Don't hesitate to do comparison shopping. Check on the nature and extent of programs and relative costs.

2. Regard with caution job counseling firms which dazzle you with self-serving statistics and pie-in-the-sky promises to put you on the road to a dream job.

3. Don't yield to high pressure tactics, no matter how convincing. Don't let them intimidate you.

4. Check with your local Better Business Bureau or the Department of Consumer Affairs for any complaints against the firm.

5. Know in advance the length of the program you're paying for and just what it includes. Are there any extras or hidden costs that may be sprung on you as you proceed with the program?

6. Check if the firm has a refund policy, should you for whatever reason decide to discontinue with the program.

7. Find out how long the firm has been in business under its present name and in its present location.

8. Before signing up, get to meet the counselor who will be your mentor. Find out how long he's been with the firm, his credentials, and whether he'll be working with you for the entire length of the program.

9. Take time to read the contract carefully. If it's an expensive venture, check with an attorney familiar with such matters.

10. Have them show you a list of clients you may want to contact to verify boastful claims made by the firm. Don't take "it's confidential" for an answer.

WHERE THE JOBS ARE

REACHING THE HIDDEN JOB MARKET

Did you know that an overwhelming number of the best jobs are rarely publicly advertised? This figure is estimated to be 80%. It may even be higher. Consequently, the vast pool of non-advertised job openings lies undetected in the hidden job market, sadly overlooked by the average job seeker. Yet that's where the bulk of the choice jobs are. Networking is one way of reaching that hidden job market; "cold-turkey" calling is another.

Networking

Broadly speaking, networking involves compiling a roster of people you know—relatives, friends, associates, whomever, who in turn know other people who likewise know others, thus enlarging by geometric progression the number of prospects to follow up. One person is a link to another, one source leads to another, and so on. Theoretically, the more people you get to know and make it your business to contact, the better your chances for tracking down the job you are looking for.

Networking can be a magic tool in an innovative job hunt. It opens unmarked doors of opportunity for you through personal contacts and referrals. It presupposes, and rightfully so, that most people, regardless of their professional rank or station in life, feel flattered when approached for advice and are willing—sometimes eager—to extend a helping hand to someone else. It makes them feel good about themselves and enhances their self-image and sense of importance. Virtue is its own reward. Less altruistically, it may provide them with a looked-for opportunity to repay a past favor or anticipate one in return sometime in the future.

Networking gets into first gear when you sit down to compile a comprehensive list of people you are (or have previously been) associated with, professionally or otherwise. Here is an organized plan for setting up such a networking system.

On a large sheet of paper write down as many names of people you know as might suggest themselves to you. The more, the better. At this stage there is no need to be overly concerned whether those on your list will turn out to be helpful or not in your job search. Right now your task is to develop a nucleus from which your network will spread out. It helps to subdivide the basic list into categories such as the following:

Family members, friends and neighbors: parents, wife/husband, brothers, sisters, uncles, aunts, cousins, in-laws, and the collective circle of friends and neighbors.

Professional service contacts: doctors, dentists, lawyers, accountants, banking officials, stockbrokers, real estate agents, insurance agents, mechanics, etc.

Business acquaintances: former employers and co-workers, department supervisors, competitors, clients, people in your general line of work.

Political and civic leaders: elected officials as well as those running for office, for whom you actively campaigned—local councilmen, state senators, and those higher up in the political arena. People you know from volunteer work with the United Way, the Heart Fund, the Red Cross, and various local charity drives.

Religious affiliates: clergymen, lay members of your congregation, members of the Men's Club, Sisterhood, people with whom you have served on various committees.

Social and avocational acquaintances: fellow members of the Knights of Pythias, Knights of Columbus, Masonic Lodge, B'nai B'rith; members of self-improvement groups such as Dale Carnegie Seminars, Young Executive Club, Toastmasters; people you've gotten to know through the "Y" and various adult education classes. Also golf cronies, tennis partners, members of the bowling team, athletic club you belong to.

School contacts: present and former instructors, long-time school chums, members of the alumni, sorority and fraternity, advisory commission. Include placement and guidance personnel.

This compilation could end up with 30 or 40 names, maybe more. When completed, the next step is to carefully review all the names and select five people who are not only known to be highly informed about the job market as it concerns you, but are in a position to help you along the way in your job hunt. It's not to be expected that you will be handed a job outright (although that's a possibility) but that they will be amenable to be approached for authoritative information and advice. The next step is to contact each one individually. If it develops that they can refer you to a job prospect that you could follow up or go as far as to help set up an appointment for you, that would be a lucky break indeed. However, if they are unable to offer you the assistance you seek in this respect, ask each of them in turn to suggest four or five others who might possibly be in a position to help you. Likewise follow up these referrals the same way.

With continued effort, it is conceivable that the selected list of five will grow in ever-increasing numbers to build up a personal directory of sources you can contact for information about where the jobs are.

That's what networking is all about!

Cold Turkey Job Hunting

The term ''cold turkey'' is slang of unknown origin and has varied meanings and applications. In selling, it means making the rounds of potential customers, often without an appointment. The initial contact with a prospect can be established by phoning him, sending him a sales letter, or straightaway walking into his office with a good sales pitch and/or samples. In an aggressive job hunt, it has the same meaning, except here you are not selling a company product or service, you are selling yourself as a would-be employee. The prospect is not a customer; he is a potential employer.

Cold turkey calling puts you in a class by yourself. You are not competing with others for an existing job opening publicized through the usual channels; you are surveying prospective employment opportunities on a much broader and less competitive plane. Whereas in networking you start off by compiling a list of people you know personally (friends, family, current and past associates, etc.), here your task is to compile a list of people you *don't* know—people whose names you have come across through a variety of sources: the business section of newspapers, trade journals, reference directories of all kinds (including the phone book), annual reports, chance meetings at conventions, trade shows, and professional seminars.

Cold turkey job hunting is not for the timid. You must be an aggressive person with the skin of a rhinoceros not to be squelched by having the door closed in your face or rejected by more subtle means. Perseverance is the key to success in cold turkey calling, as any commission salesman will tell you, but the opportunity for success makes it all worthwhile. Nothing may happen for weeks on end, and then, if your endurance holds out, you hit a gold nugget. You are the very person the company was hoping to get and the job is the one you had been dreaming about all along, but were almost in despair of ever finding.

In a broad sense, the cold turkey technique is not confined to legwork or telephoning. It includes the more traditional vehicle of making job contacts—that is, mailing out unsolicited letters of application and resumes to companies you have researched as being the most promising prospects for a person with your qualifications.

Cold turkey job hunt techniques and networking are by no means mutually exclusive; indeed, they are linked in a joint program to penetrate the hidden job market.

HOW TO PREPARE A RESUME
TO SHOW YOU OFF
AT YOUR BEST

CONFLICTING OPINIONS ABOUT THE VALUE OF A RESUME

According to some employment consultants, resumes are a sheer waste of time and money—both of which can be channeled to a more productive phase of the total job-search campaign. Indeed, John Truitt, founder of a national chain of 800 independent recruiters, says, "in some instances a resume can be more of a hindrance than a help." Others, like Richard Nelson Bolles, author of the popular *What Color is Your Parachute?*, are more conciliatory. A resume, Bolles is willing to grant, can serve a useful purpose if you don't bank on it too much—if you don't regard it a "salvation from heaven." Then there's the other side. There are those who claim, without any if's and but's, that a resume is an important credential for anyone looking for a job. It is a passport to an interview. Here is what the owner of a leading New York employment agency has to say about the subject: "I won't bother considering a job applicant unless he or she presents a resume or is willing to prepare one."

If the experts don't agree, where does that leave you, the job seeker? To reach your own conclusion, all you have to do is look through the classified ads in any large city newspaper or trade publication. You'll see that the majority of better-paying positions advertised suggest or actually specify that a resume be included with the letter of application. Of course, nobody forces you to comply, but nonetheless it's what employers are asking for.

It's true that a resume is not needed for a variety of routine or low-paying jobs. If you happen to be an itinerant dishwasher out of work and come across a "Dishwasher Wanted" sign posted in the window of Sloppy Joe's Diner, you'll need no fancy resume to apply, or if you are an experienced bartender with no itchy fingers, can stay sober, and if the job is open—it can be yours without the formality of a resume. But if you identify yourself as a career-minded individual aspiring to a managerial or executive position, you should know this: Based on my many years of experience in career guidance, I am fully in accord with those who say that a resume unquestionably improves your chances to get the job you want. Let's put it on a more personal level. If I were interested in securing a position in my field of specialization, I would not hesitate to include a resume in a letter of application, and would be sure to have one in my folder when going to an interview.

"Did a resume help you get the job you now hold?," was one of the questions that appeared in a survey of 1000 job holders who had prepared a resume and made

ANNE GRAPPONE

342 East 62 Street, New York, N.Y. 10018 ··· 838-3501

March 4, 1987

Mr. Edward Rondthaler, President
Photo-Lettering Inc.
216 East 45th Street
New York, New York 10017

Dear Mr. Rondthaler:

Our mutual friend, Bob (Doc) Leslie, whom I met at the Typophile Club recently, mentioned that you are planning to enlarge your art department to include a specialist in calligraphy.

From the enclosed resume you will see why Bob thought it a good idea to contact you and why he feels strongly that you will be interested in a person with my qualifications. As you'll note, I graduated with top honors from the Rhode Island School of Design four years ago and have since worked on a freelance basis creating logotypes and calligraphic designs for leading packaging houses and advertising agencies.

At this point in time, Mr. Rondthaler, I would like to associate myself with an organization such as yours on a permanent basis. With that in mind, I will take the liberty to call your secretary early next week to see what arrangements can be made for us to meet.

You name the day and time; I'll be there.

Sincerely yours,

Anne Grappone

Anne Grappone

EXAMPLE OF REFERRAL LETTER

use of it in their job search. Fully 90% of those who answered said "definitely yes." Similar surveys show beyond a doubt that a well-written, properly presented resume is a decided asset in any job hunt. A job applicant who has a resume has an advantage over those of his competitors who are unprepared in this respect.

TYPES OF RESUMES

There are three basic types: Chronological resume, Functional resume, and Curriculum Vitae.

A *chronological resume* is one which lists in sequential fashion highlights of work experience and educational background in year-by-year reverse order, starting from the most recent and going back in time. This type of resume is mostly favored by those who have a history of fairly continuous employment in one line of work, with no conspicuous time-gaps between jobs.

A *functional resume*, by contrast, stresses general work skills acquired during the years, without giving emphasis to specific dates of employment. This type of resume permits greater latitude to divert attention from a history of miscellaneous jobs and skills not targeted to one specific career objective. It is recommended for those who have been self-employed or have worked as a consultant or freelancer and for those entering the job market for the first time or after a long absence.

A *curriculum vitae* represents a blend of the chronological and functional resumes and is reserved mainly for persons in the academic fields as well as in the professions of law, medicine, and the sciences. As such, it features a scholarly background documented with universities attended, degrees earned, professional achievements, affiliations, published works, and a listing of positions held in specialized fields.

Your choice of resume will depend largely on your job objective, your background, and your professional status.

THE ANATOMY OF A RESUME

A resume is in effect a summary sheet in outline form with key headings which include Job Objective, Work Experience, Educational Background, Personal Data, and often as not, References, though not necessarily in this sequence.

Job Objective

This phase of the resume has always been and probably will remain a controversial issue among job counselors and professional resume writers. Some stand firm in the belief that a Job Objective should *always* be stated somewhere on a resume. Their argument is that the omission of a job objective forces the employer to deduce from the body of the resume just what the candidate's career goal is,

BARBARA HOLLINGSWORTH
250 Riverside Drive
New York, NY 10039
(212) 369-7880

. . . .

OBJECTIVE:	Administrative Assistant to busy Executive.
QUALIFICATIONS AND EXPERIENCE:	Best expressed in the words of an ad my supervisor placed in the classified section of WOMEN'S WEAR DAILY, upon my giving notice that I intend to resign as soon as he can find a replacement.

> "I am losing my Best Girl. She
> types like a dream, takes dictation faster
> than I can talk, handles clients with tact
> and diplomacy, does library research,
> thinks, works under pressure, and
> SMILES."

	My total work experience since finishing college three years ago has been with one company, Smithline Associates, 385 Madison Avenue, New York City--a fashion advertising agency employing 30 people. Reason for leaving: To diversify my experience in area of administration and management.
EDUCATION:	Pace College, New York City, 1981 - 1984. A.A. degree in Secretarial Studies. H.S. Music & Art, New York City, 1979 - 1981. A average. Punctuality and Attendance Award.
PERSONAL:	Born 1961: Height 5'5": Weight 122 lbs. Appearance: well groomed, considered attractive. Happy outlook on life.
AFFILIATIONS:	Corresponding Secretary, Advertising Club of New York; Member, Advertising Women's Production Club; Member, Promotion Committee, local chapter of the United Way.
REFERENCES:	My present employer.

. . . .

EXAMPLE OF ONE-PAGE CHRONOLOGICAL RESUME

DOROTHY KENNY

10 PARK RD., STORRS, CONN. 10671 · (203) 771-1121

R E S U M E

CAREER OBJECTIVE

Executive position in strategic planning or product development focusing on newly emerging technologies of home information services, with emphasis on electronic home banking and shopping.

EXPERIENCE

7/80 - Present

20TH CENTURY TRANSFERS SYSTEMS INC., New York, New York

Executive Vice President

Promoted 7/81 from V.P., Research and Planning to Executive V.P. As chief operating officer, direct program in research and development in electronic funds transfer, home banking, strategic planning and information technology applied to the thrift industry. Responsible for a budget of $350,000 program development and membership liaison.

Developed a timesharing-based decision support system for financial planning, currently utilized by 20 thrift institutions. This system was selected by the FDIC to be utilized in monitoring and evaluating the financial performance of the approximately 325 savings banks under its jurisdiction.

Initiated the development of new products and prepared business plans for new ventures to increase service revenues for banking institutions.

7/78 - 6/80

CARLSON CONTAINER CORP., White Plains, New York

Director, Corporate Planning

Member of Management Committee, which sets company policy, directs overall business activities and evaluates key issues of market strategy.

Directed a strategic planning study to develop projections of long term market growth in the global container leasing industry, leading to a 28% increase in capital budget allocations for new equipment.

Revised approach to pricing damage protection insurance to avoid potential annual loss of $1.5 million with self-insurance.

EXAMPLE OF TWO-PAGE CHRONOLOGICAL RESUME

Analyzed operational performance of leased equipment leading to a change in depreciation policy which increased net income more than $2 million in the first year.

10/73 - 10/78

S.T. SPENCER ASSOCIATES, New York, New York

Internal Consultant, Financial Services Division

Designed financial information systems for planning, budgeting and reporting.

Directed development of an English-like computer timesharing language for use by financial analysts, which has been profitably marketed by a commerical timesharing service on a royalty basis since 1977.

Developed a set of models for financial planning and portfolio management for a public Real Estate Investment Trust with assets exceeding $50 million.

Performed a risk analysis to evaluate a proposed mining acquisition resulting in a $12 million investment.

9/72 - 9/73

Academic appointment, then staff positions with INTERNATIONAL MINERALS AND CHEMICAL CO. and DUNLAP AND ASSOCIATES.

EDUCATION

Johns Hopkins Univ., Ph.D., Engineering, major in Operations Research, 1971.

Univ. of Toronto, B.Sc., Aeronautical Engineering, 1966.

PROFESSIONAL AFFILIATIONS

North American Society for Corporate Planning
The Institute of Management Sciences
American Statistical Association
Sigma X1, national scientific honorary
Included in WHO'S WHO OF AMERICAN WOMEN - 13th edition

EXAMPLE OF CHRONOLOGICAL RESUME (CONTINUED)

or what position he is applying for. It could very well be that the candidate himself doesn't know—and that, by the way, is not at all uncommon.

You're better off, others aver, *not* to list a Job Objective as a separate heading. This permits your would-be employer greater flexibility in considering you for any number of peripheral positions that your experience qualifies you for. Defer mentioning your job objective, they say, until a face-to-face interview materializes. Unfortunately, this advice doesn't take into account the possibility that you may not be invited to an interview in the first place if a job objective is not clearly indicated anywhere on the resume.

It is my considered opinion that, with few exceptions, a stated objective on a resume is a plus factor. It could do no harm and could do you a lot of good. Used as a focal point, the Job Objective should in 40 words or less state the position you're looking for in terms of your qualifications, as for example:

> Hands-on executive with more than 10 years of increasingly responsible business experience in the transportation-oriented industry seeks position in same with a firm planning to expand its service nationwide.

A Job Objective stands out best when it's worded like a situation wanted ad—brief and to the point. It should highlight one or two of the candidate's qualifications and motivate the prospective employer to read the rest of the resume.

Work Experience

This is a record of the jobs you've held. Unless you've had many jobs within a short period of time (making you seem like a migratory worker), each job listed should show date of employment, name of firm, job title, responsibilities, and accomplishments. Reason for leaving need not be included. That matter is best deferred to the actual interview, if the subject comes up.

It should be borne in mind that the prospective employer, while interested in an overview of your entire employment history, will pay particular attention to your most recent job—the one which presumably represents your highest level of achievement. This should be the most detailed.

Date of Employment: The duration of employment for each job should be indicated on a year-to-year basis. There is no need to specify months. However, if your work experience includes a series of short-term jobs—as in the case of part-time or summer work—these can be listed by months.

Firms: When listing firms you worked for, no exact address need be given. Just the city and state will do. You may mention the nature of a firm's products or services and the position it holds among its competitors, space permitting.

Job Title: This refers to your payroll position—Programmer/Analyst, Production Supervisor, Credit Manager, etc.

Responsibilities: Here you briefly describe the duties of each position held. A job title in itself does not indicate the extent of your responsibilities. For example: Manager, Claims Department, may mean managing a department of two, or fifty.

If you were in charge of a large department, it is to your advantage to give the actual number of people involved.

Accomplishments: Merely mentioning responsibilities does not tell the complete story. What is important is to show how you carried out these responsibilities measured as by productivity and company profits. When that is not feasible, mention other records of achievements such as special awards and citations, commendations by supervisors, or promotion to higher rank.

If you state that you introduced an innovative idea or system, that is commendable, but remember that you must show how it turned out to benefit the company. It is conceivable that your efforts could very well have been so foolhardy as to have proven disastrous to your company, and in fact explains why you no longer work there. In the last analysis, it's the *result*, not the effort, that determines the success of a venture.

Educational Background

This heading may include a list of schools attended, with dates for each, degrees and honors earned, and noteworthy participation in extracurricular activities. The details here will vary with the extent of your educational background. As a college graduate with a string of degrees, you need not bother tabulating courses taken in your early school years. On the other hand, someone with a limited education will find it advantageous to list those courses which are job-oriented.

Personal Data

This may include physical statistics (height, weight, health) as well as age, hobbies, community activities and professional affiliations.

Physical statistics: Use your own good judgment on how much space—if any—to allow to this phase of Personal Data, unless of course you are in show business, a high fashion model, or anyone else applying for a position where physical statistics bear special relevance to the job. Go ahead and mention your 6′2′′, 185 lb. muscular physique if you feel it will help you get the job as security officer, bodyguard, or chief bouncer in a honky-tonk nightclub. If you enjoy good health, you may state it without making it look like a medical report.

Age or Date of Birth: If at forty or thereabouts you have to date not earned accolades as an outstanding achiever, it is unwise to state your age. (I have seen any number of resumes with the interviewer's marginal notation, "over the hill" or similar epithet.) While enlightened Personnel Directors are not averse to hiring people in their forties and beyond in the knowledge that they are reputed to have greater stability and stick-to-it-iveness, and are less frequently absent or late, there still exists a residual bias against "older" workers. By the same token, if you are angling for a position which is definitely youth-oriented—advertising, for example—and you identify yourself with that age group, then there is good reason for you to state your age. In every case it's a matter of personal discretion to decide whether or not to make reference to age.

STEVEN C. CHAN / 22 ASHTON ST., ALLSTON, MASS. 02134 / 522-1245

April 10, 1987

Mr. Larry Rosten, President
Urban Image Corporation
253 Summer Street
Boston, Mass. 13234

Dear Mr. Rosten:

    Recently I spoke with Charlie Hoyt of September Productions. In our conversation he mentioned that you would be an interesting person to speak to about the film and broadcasting industry.

    As a recent graduate of Boston University film department, I am at the point in my career where I must make a decision about my future. I have experience in several artistic disciplines and would ultimately like to produce, direct and write documentary and commercial films. As you no doubt surmise, I must explore these prospects thoroughly and devise some type of career strategy. This is one reason I would like to talk with you. With the expertise you have in film, your advice and insight about the industry would be very beneficial to me.

    By talking to you I would like to gain information on how you launched your career, what problems and obstacles you came up against, what important issues and problems exist in the industry, how the Boston job market compares to national prospects in the field, and what ideas and suggestions you may have as to how I can launch my career.

    I've included a resume only for the purpose of giving you some insight into my interests, abilities, potential and experience. Let me assure you that by giving you a resume I am not seeking a job from you. I am only seeking advice and information about the field in order to sharpen my perspective. If you could help me out in this respect I would greatly appreciate it.

    I'll phone you early next week to find out when I could have the privilege of meeting with you.

Sincerely,

Steven C. Chan

Steven C. Chan

EXAMPLE OF PERSONALIZED COVER LETTER

313 Grand Concourse
Bronx, NY 10468
Phone: 872-9361

May 12, 1987

Mr. William Binder, President
Metropolitan Art Agency
485 Lexington Avenue
New York, NY 10021

Dear Mr. Binder:

Here is my story:

66 My name is Harry Gittleman. I am a seventeen-year-old
commercial art major with little experience, but lots
of potential.

Next month I will be graduating from high school and am
lining up a job in advance. I have also contacted three
other good firms for which I would like to work, but I
would be happiest working for yours. I am ready to meet
with you any time after school hours. 99

Sincerely,

Harry Gittleman
Harry Gittleman

EXAMPLE OF UNCONVENTIONAL LETTER OF APPLICATION

DAVID KAYE, M.D.
120 West 68th Street
New York, NY 10036
758-3869

PROFESSIONAL GOAL

Opportunity to participate in an urban
program which provides good medical care
to the indigent and underprivileged.

EDUCATIONAL BACKGROUND

1968 - 1972:   Columbia University, New York; B.A. degree

1972 - 1976:   Mt. Sinai School of Medicine, New York; M.D. degree.

1976 - 1977:   Beth Israel Hospital, New York; Rotating Internship.

1977 - 1980:   Roosevelt Hospital, New York; Three-year Residency.
                   2 years --- Internal Medicine
                   1 year ---- Hematology

PROFESSIONAL BACKGROUND

1982 - 1983:   Out-patient Clinic, ILGWU Medical Center, New York.
                   Served as examining physician for union
                   members and their dependents.

1983 - Date: Equitable Life Insurance Company, New York.
                   Examining physician, life insurance
                   applicants. Medical evaluations,
                   routine and cardiovascular cases.

MILITARY SERVICE

1980 - 1982:   Captain, Army Medical Corps: Fort Carson, Colorado.
                   Primarily in-patient service at base
                   hospital with 6 to 8 hours per week
                   out-patient duty. Honorable discharge,
                   Sept. 1982. No further military obli-
                   gations.

PERSONAL INFORMATION

Age: 32   Height: 5'10"   Weight: 170 lbs.
Health: Top shape   Married, no children   Vision: 20/20

Currently in process of preparing for boards in internal medicine.

EXAMPLE OF CURRICULUM VITAE

Marital status: You may state whether you are single or married. If widowed, divorced, or separated, there is nothing to be gained by calling attention to it in the resume. For all practical purposes, if you are not married, you are single.

Military experience: If you have put in a stint in the armed services, this should be mentioned, together with the length of service, to account for the obvious time gap in your work history. Also, if you have risen in the ranks, it may serve your purpose to make brief reference to it as evidence of leadership potential.

Hobbies: Don't use precious space on the resume cataloging hobbies unless they in some way reflect your job objective. You're into astrology? Forget it! How does that relate to the Director of Marketing Communications position you're after?

When uncertain whether your pet hobby or other avocational interest should be included or not, the rule is "If in doubt, leave it out."

Community Activities and Professional Organizations: In some instances, it is desirable to list civic and community organizations in which you play an active role. This would normally apply to such fields as insurance, real estate, and finance, where the larger the circle of people you come in contact with, the greater your scope of operation. Remember: "Every friend is a potential customer."

Don't let modesty stand in your way from listing affiliations with professional organizations in your field of work. Also, there's no reason why you should not mention articles you may have written for trade or professional journals, or your participation in technical forums, or anything of the kind that you feel will enhance your status as a candidate.

References

This heading can be left out completely to conserve space. Any seasoned interviewer knows well enough that candidates will only list favorable references. You may, if you wish, briefly note, "References on hand," or "References to be supplied at the interview."

PHYSICAL MAKE-UP AND APPEARANCE OF RESUME

It takes so much time and effort to develop a job-getting resume that it would be foolish to stint on the cost of paper and quality of printing. "Good paper makes a good impression" is a well-known slogan in the paper industry. High-quality stock may cost a little more, but it yields better printing results, thus enhancing the total appearance of the finished resume.

Traditionally, resumes are printed on 8½" x 11" bond paper. White is best, but a subtle tint of gray or beige can be effective. Discretion must be exercised when to depart from the standard size and color of stock. Odd sizes and exotic colors can make the resume look like a sentimental missive—not like a business data sheet, which it really is. Regardless of the color of stock, the printing ink should not depart from black, which is easiest to read.

STEVEN C. CHAN / 22 ASHTON ST., ALLSTON, MASS. 02134 / 522-1245

CAREER OBJECTIVE

To use my communicative, artistic abilities and my knowledge of film equipment to assist in script development, filming, and editing for a production house or independent filmmaker.

PRODUCTION SKILLS

Co-producer, Director, Cinematographer and Editor for a commercially sold 12-minute documentary film about the attempted occupation of the Seabrook Nuclear Power Plant in Maine on 8/10/81.

Assistant Cameraman for Dave Comtois' short dramatic film, IN PASSING. Responsible for camera maintenance, loading, logging shots, reading light, setting aperture, pulling focus, shot set-ups, and crowd control.

Assistant Editor and Production Assistant for Michael Korolenko's feature-length, dramatic documentary-musical, CHORDS OF FAME, a-bout the life of Phil Ochs. Responsible for picking up and delivering sound transfers and dailies, synching up dailies, keeping an assembly log, recording order, edge, and roll numbers, assembling preferred takes for screening. Set design, lighting set-up, extra sign-ups, crowd control, cue cards, van rentals, quiet set, and slating.

ARTISTIC SKILLS

Theater Scholarship at Pennsylvania Governor's School for the Arts. Selected for a $1000 summer acting scholarship. Improved ability and understanding of effective speech and movements; honed esthetic eye for composition, movement and lighting. In addition to acting and directing, gained experience and knowledge of stagecraft and makeup.

Sculpture - National Gold Medal. As one of thirty-one sculptures chosen from 150,000 national entrees in the Scholastic Art Competition, my artistic talent, ability to translate ideas into physical representation, artistic dexterity and my esthetic eye for space, composition, and form were affirmed.

Animator for John Ketchner's and Bill Arntz's dramatic feature-length film, BEAT THE DEVA. Responsible for animation design, airbrushing and rotoscoping. Participated in the creative process for and shooting of the animation stills.

EDUCATIONAL BACKGROUND

Boston Univ., B.S. In Broadcasting and Film, Minor in Marketing

EMPLOYMENT RECORD AND REFERENCES ON REQUEST

EXAMPLE OF FUNCTIONAL RESUME

A resume should be neatly typed, devoid of any evidence of erasures, corrections, or other signs of a struggle. If you're not a good typist, get it done professionally. Since multiple copies are needed in any protracted job-hunt, the original or master copy must be flawless. A print can only be as good as the original.

To look esthetically good and at the same time be easy to read, the wording should be arranged into thought groups or blocks of copy under each main heading, with an effort made to allow plenty of marginal white space. This is not easy. Undoubtedly it will be necessary for you to redo the resume many times. Even professional resume writers can spend hours revising the wording and jockeying the various blocks of copy until a pleasing typographic relationship is established among them. Though it is desirable to get the wording to fit on a single page, there is no hard-and-fast rule about that. In some instances, a two- or even a three-page resume is an acceptable alternative.

COMMON FAULTS IN RESUME PREPARATION

The following is a compilation of statements underscoring common faults in resume preparation which explain why so many job resumes end up in the interviewer's wastepaper basket, rather than the active file.

- *Fails to include pertinent facts*: The resume reads like an autobiography. Too much space is given over to non-important points of information at the expense of those aspects which bear a direct relation to the applicant's work history and experience.

- *Irrelevancies and flowery language*: The resume is replete with personal opinions and editorial commentaries on life and society. Emotionally-tinged statements such as, "It has always been my fervent hope that ——," "In our industrial jungle of dog-eat-dog ——," "Vast horizons of our new frontier," are out of place in a job resume, appropriate as they may be in an essay or editorial.

- *Broad generalizations with no back-up*: All talk but no show. To say, "I had a highly successful selling record" is a bland, self-serving statement. Any such claims must be supported by concrete evidence to be meaningful. A more objective way of putting it would be, "During the last three years with the company, my sales increased more than 20% each year. Upon leaving, my annual sales record was greater than any of the other six salesmen who had been with the company a longer time."

- *Overselling former employer or company*: Just as it isn't cricket to knock a former employer, it is pointless to glorify him.

- *Lack of definite career goal*: The applicant is evidently not clear in his own mind what job he is looking for or what career he wants to pursue.

- *Evidence of job hopping*: Too many short-duration jobs listed, indicating a lack of stability. The applicant appears to be a drifter.

- *Too much self-praise:* Self-glorification and taking credit for achievements which apparently are not entirely due to the job candidate's own efforts. Too many I's, me's, and mine's in the resume.

- *Too lengthy, too verbose:* Material could have easily been condensed to focus on facts rather than on generalities.

- *Unexplained gaps in work and educational background:* Seeming lack of continuity in applicant's history. Some years not accounted for.

- *Resume too gimmicky:* Indiscreet use of colored printing ink and fancy, odd-size paper. Exotic typefaces such as Old English and certain scripts obviously intended to make the resume look "different" end up being difficult to read.

- *Poor presentation:* Errors in spelling, grammar and punctuation; lack of consistency in wording and arrangement of copy; printing below professional standards.

In conclusion, to test how your resume will pull with a prospective employer, ask yourself, "If I were the employer reading this resume, would I want to hire me?"

A WORD ABOUT COVER LETTERS AND LETTERS OF APPLICATION

A cover letter (sometimes referred to as a transmittal letter) is a short, business-like correspondence which calls the prospective employer's attention to an enclosed resume. The purpose of a cover letter is to point up why the applicant is convinced that the qualifications he possesses are just right for the job he seeks (as summarized in the resume) and are worthy of the prospective employer's consideration. Without a cover letter, an unsolicited resume is a throwaway, and is bound to end up in the morgue files of the Personnel Department.

Basically, a letter of application is a written response to an existing job opening. It may also be used as a promotion piece showing your qualifications for a particular job or service you can render a company that you'd like to work for. Either way, it may or may not include a resume. The way it is worded should accomplish one main objective: It should sufficiently arouse the would-be employer's curiosity about you and result in an invitation to an interview.

The most readable cover letter or letter of application is one that is brief and to the point, hardly more than 200 words in length. No matter how many letters you send off, each should be typed by hand and signed, and wherever possible, directed to a particular individual by name and title.

4

HOW YOU LOOK
MAKES A DIFFERENCE

SOME TIME AGO a young lady told me she always makes an effort to look her best when speaking to her favorite boyfriend on the phone. Observing my puzzled expression, she explained that when she looks right, she feels right—is more sure of herself—a feeling which is somehow transmitted over the miles of wire that geographically separate her from her friend. This is by no means a personal eccentricity. We all know that a good appearance engenders a feeling of self-confidence and well-being. Isn't that precisely the image you want to project in a job interview?

All job applicants are tense at an interview. You are no different. But you will be unduly tense (and much more ill at ease) if you are not sure of your appearance, and thus are psychologically hindered from presenting to advantage the otherwise superior qualifications you have to offer. You are not giving yourself a fair break unless your total appearance presents you at your level best. The interview is the crucial point of your entire job hunt—just one step away from a job offer. Don't botch it up. It is the culmination of the bushelfuls of resumes you mailed out, dozens of ''cold'' contacts you made to prospective employers, the numerous agencies you registered with, the classified ads you waded through.

Before you meet the interviewer face to face, take a moment or two to look at yourself in a full-length mirror: carefully, from top to bottom. Try to see yourself objectively, just as the interviewer will, during those long 30 to 40 minutes that tick away from entrance to exit. Remember, you'll be sized up from the moment you walk through the door—and the first impression is often a lasting one, in your favor or otherwise.

Two looking-glass checklists are presented here—one for men, one for women—to make you more aware of some of the basic elements of good appearance.

"Is such a checklist really necessary?", you may be inclined to ask. "By golly, am I not mature enough to know how to dress for an interview—or for any occasion—without having to refer to an itemized checklist?"

Kid stuff, you say? The fact remains that so many good applicants are turned down because of poor appearance. Interestingly enough they are usually among the ones who pooh-pooh any counseling in this respect. Even if you are fully aware of how important a role good appearance plays in an interview (as no doubt you are), a checklist in print will, I am sure, serve as a helpful reminder, if nothing more.

CHECKLIST FOR MEN

Good Grooming

Is your hair well-groomed? Your hair may have been nice and neat, just the way you wanted it to be when you started out for the session with the interviewer. It may no longer be so by the time you get there. A pocket comb and mirror will come in handy to put that stray lock of hair in place.

Is your hair well-trimmed? Unless you are a long-haired musician or rock performer, remember to get a haircut or trim in preparation for the interview. But don't step into the interviewer's office directly from the barber and smelling like it, with bits of stray hair clinging to your collar which he failed to brush off. Your visit to the barber needn't be that recent!

Is your hair clean and free from dandruff? Perhaps there's nothing contagious about dandruff, but it can be an unsightly nuisance—more noticeably so when it settles on a dark garment. True, while you can't effect an overnight cure for something that has baffled dermatologists for years, a good hairwash and conditioner is sure to help temporarily and will add lustre to any head of hair.

Does your hair show signs of gray? Though a touch of gray hair may add a note of distinction to a man's appearance, graying hair does tend to make one look older than his true age. Some years back I was a guest speaker at a gathering of 250 of New York's leading art directors, and at 48 I felt I was the oldest one there—or appeared to be so because of my graying hair. It is common knowledge that the business world generally and the advertising field in particular is strongly youth-oriented.

For a more youthful look, consider using a hair dye. Millions of men do. How you feel about touching up your hair depends largely on your self image.

Are you well-shaved? Take care not to nick your skin, a possibility when using a traditional razor. Blood spots on chin and neck have a way of offsetting on your shirt collar and could look terrible.

Be sure you have proper illumination. Your dressing mirror need not be surrounded by rows of bulbs like a movie star's makeup table, but you do need sufficient light to see what you're doing.

A close shave gives you a neat appearance and a younger look. This takes on greater importance when you arrive at a period in life when your hair shows signs of graying. As you get older you have to make an extra effort to put your best (and youngest) face forward.

Hint: If you have lined up more than one interview for the same day, shave again if there is an appreciable time lapse between one interview and the next. Ted Kennedy is said to shave several times a day (and change shirts as often) when scheduled to attend a number of public functions on the same day.

How are your hands and nails? Look at your hands. The interviewer will. Your hands are one of the prime focal spots from the interviewer's vantage point. Be sure they are immaculately clean. Though your nails need not have a glitzy polish, they should be properly trimmed and shaped.

Basic Wardrobe

Is your suit right for the occasion? When interviewed for any office or professional job, you'll not go wrong if you exercise conservative taste in dress. A dark blue or gray suit carries the mark of success in the business world. For executive or managerial positions, a three-piece dark suit has by custom become fairly standard; for lower ranking positions, a two-piece suit is acceptable.

Everybody is acquainted with the inherent advantages of clothing made of polyester. It doesn't crease easily, is spot removable, machine washable, and requires little or no pressing. You can be sure that any connoisseur of fine quality clothing can recognize a red-tag-sale polyester suit a mile away. It's cheaper—and looks it!

If it's a high-ranking position you are angling for, with corresponding salary prospects, provide yourself with at least two well-tailored suits made of a balanced blend of wool and silk. Add them to your basic wardrobe and mark "to be reserved for interviews and other business occasions." A good quality suit has a soft feel to it and drapes better on the figure. A suit and the various components of a well-coordinated wardrobe should be regarded as a worthwhile investment in your career. If you want to look like a success, dress accordingly. There is a syndicated newspaper column that runs under the heading, "You Are What Your Wear" and in it this point is stressed ever so many times. Think about it!

Is your shirt appropriate? The shirt you wear will definitely be taken note of by your interviewer. Never appear wearing a shirt that's become tired from too many washings and is beginning to show signs of fraying around collar and cuffs. At the same time, don't show up wearing one that's brand new—that has never been through the laundry before. A just-bought shirt worn for the first time looks *too* new! It identifies you as someone obviously spruced up for the occasion.

Include in your wardrobe several good-quality dress shirts (white or pale blue-gray) with full-length sleeves. Short-sleeve shirts are okay for casual wear, but hardly ever acceptable when being interviewed for sales, managerial, and executive-level positions. French cuffs and cuff links add a touch of elegance to your attire.

Is your tie appropriate? Your tie, another important focal point in your wardrobe, should be spotlessly clean and free from wrinkles. Don't rely on a perfunctory brushing and patting to make stains and wrinkles go away. A modestly priced, yet clean and color-coordinated tie will do more for your appearance than a Countess Mara creation that has seen better days. Take time in knotting your tie, making sure that the knot is firmly shaped and both ends finish up at the same length. Discrete color contrast is always desirable, but contrast can easily become clash. A good example: a striped maroon tie worn with a dark gray suit makes for a pleasing color contrast, whereas a Kelly-green tie with a blue suit clashes violently.

Are your socks right for the rest of your outfit? According to the dictates of fashion, men's socks should not be of a lighter color than the trousers. Also for business and formal wear, knee high's are preferable to shorties so that your shanks are not exposed when crossing your legs. The anatomy of a man's leg is hardly ever enhanced by a peek-a-boo view of a fuzzy coating of hair. White socks are strictly for nurses and podiatrists, never for job applicants presenting themselves at an interview.

Are your shoes well-shined and in good condition? It's easier to get a good shine than to hide your feet under the chair you're sitting on. Are your soles in good condition? A hole in one is an achievement on the golf course, not so on the sole of a shoe. Do you need new heels? There is something about worn-down heels which give the wearer a shabby, rundown look. The heels of your shoes are more noticeable than you think. Remember the old O'Sullivan slogan ? "Look at your heels, everyone else does!"

Slip-on shoes originally designed for casual wear now come in a wide variety of dressy styles and are acceptable for nearly all social and business occasions. If, however, you prefer wearing shoes designed for laces, check to see that they are neatly and securely tied. Loose or dangling laces may not only give you a feeling of psychological insecurity but can literally cause you to stumble over your own feet.

"Avoid combining black shoes (laced or otherwise) with a brown suit", say the men's fashion magazines. The two make a bad combination. Whatever color or style, fine-crafted leather shoes not only wear better but look better, though they are more costly than the vinyl or other man-made synthetics. There is just no substitute for a well-polished, good quality leather shoe.

What about a topcoat? Heavyweight coats have long been phased out in preference to lightweight, all-weather "trench" coat styles which are serviceable for nearly all occasions. Presumably you won't be interviewed wearing a coat. However, even if you carry it on your arm, or the receptionist hangs it up for you, the kind and quality of coat you wear will not go unnoticed.

For some unknown reason, people seem to put greater trust in someone wearing a light-colored coat rather than a dark one. In the movies when the good guy is shown wearing a coat, it's always light, whereas the bad guy invariably is in

somber black. So, if you intend to wear a coat going to an interview, pick a light color. Show you're a good guy!

MISCELLANEOUS

WALLET

A slimline wallet will keep your pocket from bulging and help retain the natural contour of your well-tailored suit. The contents of the wallet should be limited to essentials. Don't overload it with an assortment of credit cards, family photos, and sentimental memorabilia.

WRISTWATCH

A wristwatch can be regarded not merely as a functional timepiece but an ornamental accessory. If it's within your means, the watch you wear should be a prestigious name brand of fine quality, the same as the rest of your attire. Aspiring corporate presidents don't appear for interviews wearing Mickey Mouse watches.

HANDKERCHIEF

A hand-rolled linen handkerchief, neatly folded and set in your breast pocket, adds a note of interest to any man's attire. But more important than that, before you venture forth to a job interview, don't let it slip your mind to carry a functional handkerchief. What a source of discomfort it can be to have an urgent need for a handkerchief only to discover you forgot to bring one along—especially if you have the sniffles. Not only will this put you in a most uncomfortable situation, but the person interviewing you is bound to sense your predicament and both you and he will be greatly relieved when the interview is over.

ATTACHÉ CASE

An attaché case (or fine quality folder) somehow makes you look and feel important. More than that, from a practical standpoint, it serves as a convenient carrier for your credentials: copies of your resumes, letters of commendation, printouts of sales reports, etc. There are styles to accommodate your special needs, but whichever you require, get the top of the line.

A WORD ABOUT PERSONAL HYGIENE

A job interview for most of us is an exercise in tension, and tension often manifests itself in overcharged body perspiration and can also trigger off halitosis. Though you may not be aware of this on your own person, your interviewer will. To avoid embarrassment and at the same time put yourself out of the running as a potential candidate, take every precaution to minimize these conditions. Make it a part of your morning routine to shower thoroughly and use deodorant and mouth-wash unstintingly before going to an interview.

To sum it all up: While it is probably alright to come decked out in a brand-new suit, it is unlikely that the discerning eye of your interviewer will fail to notice that you are also breaking in a brand-new pair of shoes (soles still unsullied), a just-bought shirt, a spanking new tie—all that, plus a fresh haircut and dazzling manicure. You'll present an image of a mannequin come to life, leading your interviewer to wonder what you really look like when you're not on display.

CHECKLIST FOR WOMEN

The checklist that follows is meant to serve as a flexible guide only, since women's fashions change so frequently—often quite radically—from year to year. When selecting clothes for job interviews, the momentary whims of fashion should always take a back seat to a commonsense wardrobe that compliments your personality. When it's a high-level position you're after, splash a little. It pays to dress as expensively as you can possibly afford. In the world of business, appearance is the hallmark of success. It's not only what you know that counts, but the visual impression you make.

A thought about color coordination: It's hard to look dashing (or even interesting) in monochrome—brown dress, brown shoes (with hose to match), brown purse, brown scarf—or any other one-color scheme top to bottom. Be more daring. Introduce some point of color contrast to your ensemble.

Basic Wardrobe

Are your clothes appropriate for a business appointment which in fact a job interview really is? John T. Molloy, acknowledged dean of business wear and author of *"The Woman's Dress for Success Book"* says, "to project a successful image, start by wearing what is commonly considered serious clothing." If you are a young graduate fresh out of school, this rules out dingy blue jeans, oversized turtleneck sweaters, screen-printed T-shirts and sandals. Such informal attire may look cute or impish on campus but is out of sync in a business office. Dressing more conservatively will help you make the leap from school to a job, and you'll be taken more seriously as a prospective candidate for whatever position you apply for.

At any age, a well-fitted, tailored suit, dress or coordinated skirt and blouse with matching accessories can make you look and feel more self-confident and convey a favorable impression on the person interviewing you. Splash a little—buy the finest quality clothes you can afford.

Here are a few hints suggested by those who know good tailoring to guide you in selecting the type of garment construction that wears best and looks best: straight seams with even stitching; finished seams with no raw edges in evidence; plaids and stripes that match at the seams; even hemlines; zippers that lie flat; buttonholes that line up with buttons evenly, and with no loose threads.

If you are somewhat hippy with a large bustline, stay away from short jackets, two-piece dresses, and high flap pockets which tend to accentuate these dimensions.

Avoid skin-tight sweaters, revealing decolletage, and peek-a-boo slit skirts, if you wish to be considered for the job based solely on merit.

Are your shoes in harmony with your general ensemble? Select shoes which conform in color and style to your ensemble. For interviews, avoid spike heels even if they happen to be in vogue at the time. Shoes with medium heels are suggested because they provide a firmer and more assured step—a mark of authority for the career-bound woman.

Designer-style boots have a jaunty look about them. If you feel they go well with your ensemble (and your personality) the most flattering effect is achieved when the hem of the skirt just covers the top of the boot. A gap between hem and boot top interrupts the vertical line of your profile.

Are your hose the right shade and free from runs? Fashion stylists agree that neutral skin colors are more appropriate for businesswear than those of deeper tints.

As a precautionary measure, it's good to have a standby pair in your handbag, should the hose you're wearing develop a run en route to the interview, making a changeover necessary.

One more point. No matter how proud you may be of your legs, never show up for an interview stockingless, regardless of the job you are applying for.

Accessories

Handbag: As an important component of your ensemble, a handbag should be selected with the same care and good taste as everything else you wear. Rather than overstuffing it, make use of an attaché case as an auxiliary carrier.

Note: Avoid an oversized bag if you are on the short side of 5'3'' and a wee bit dumpy. The disproportionate contrast can only accentuate this unflattering aspect of your appearance.

Hat: Whether you decide to wear a hat or not is a matter of personal discretion. If you think a hat goes well with your ensemble (and your mirror confirms it), select one that's neither frilly nor flamboyant, but rather on the modest and more conservative side. Alluring veils and floppy, wide-brimmed chapeaus, though flattering, can be distracting in a business environment.

Jewelry: You don't feel fully dressed without jewelry and ornamental trinkets? Okay, but don't overdo it. Less is best. This means no multiple brooches, yards of reflective gold chains, jumbo-sized rings (one on each finger), and your entire collection of wrist bracelets. Exercise moderation in the size of your earrings and leave your ankle bracelet at home.

Good Grooming

Is your hairdo right for you? In general, high-styled coiffures are not recommended for job interviews, unless, of course, the job you are applying for relates specifically to professional hairstyling, fashion modeling, and the like.

Go easy on those artificially-created ringlets and studied curliques. They show an undue fastidiousness with hairdos and hint at narcissistic self-pampering. At no time come to an interview looking as if you just got through a four-hour session at your favorite hairdresser.

Are you endowed with a bountiful head of hair which in your school days you wore loose, untied, and long enough to cascade down to a little south of the midriff? Lucky you! If you can't get yourself to trim it to a more moderate length, you'll do better if you put up your tresses in a bun or some other upsweep arrangement—at least for the interview.

About a wig: A wig that looks as if ordered from a Sears catalog will call attention to itself. You're fooling no one but yourself. A well-fitted, high-quality wig can run into hundreds of dollars. It may be worth it if it truly enhances your appearance. If wearing a wig doesn't do anything for you, why let it sit on your head?

Is your makeup right for the occasion? As in hairstyling, stop short of excesses and theatricalities. Your interviewer will be sitting no more than several feet away from you, and at that close a range heavily applied makeup looks hard.

An inordinate use of mascara, oversized false lashes, and fluorescent lip rouge are out of place in a business office. Don't overdo the eyeshadow bit. Keep away from highly chromatic colors that appear blatant, especially under harsh office illumination. Eyeshadow is complimentary only if it accentuates your eyes in a natural way.

Before presenting yourself, take a moment to check your makeup to see that nothing has gone awry on the way to the interview.

Are you proud of your hands and nails? A woman's hands can be regarded as an expression of femininity. To be attractive, hands should be meticulously clean, fingernails well-manicured but never of Dragon-lady length to interfere with efficient performance of normal office routines.

Do the glasses you wear enhance or detract from your appearance? If you've been wearing the traditional kind, why not try one of the newer designer styles? They are more expensive, to be sure, but they are smarter looking and make you smarter looking too.

Never show up to an interview with sunglasses, or worse still, wearing the reflective-mirror type where the person looking at you can only see a dual reflection of his own image. Should it bother you to wear glasses of any kind, yet can't do without them, the solution may be contact lenses. More and more men and women in all walks of life are switching to contact lenses which are as functional as frame-type glasses, but are not discernible even at close range and may even improve your vision. You may not be aware of it, but many of your favorite stage and screen stars wear contact lenses, and so do ever so many celebrities in the public eye (no pun intended.) You'll be in good company!

Personal Hygiene

Everybody knows that proper care in personal hygiene is indispensable for that extra confidence that comes with a clean, fresh feeling. You can easily spoil the effect of your otherwise exemplary appearance (and be the last to realize it) if your daily routine does not include a shower, change of underwear, and use of deodorant and mouthwash. Surely there are enough TV commercials spewed out every hour of the day to remind all of us of the importance of this, the most intimate phase of good grooming. As mentioned earlier, these precautions apply to men as well.

5

CORRECTIVE MEASURES
TO IMPROVE YOUR SPEECH

FAULTY SPEECH HABITS, glaring mispronunciations, use of clichés, poor voice projection, fractured grammar, and, quite often, personal idiosyncracies in speech pattern can hold you back from getting the job you are otherwise qualified for. It's not easy to rid yourself of poor speech habits acquired through the years, and even less easy to overcome certain speech impediments. To succeed, you must first become aware of any such shortcomings, and second do something about correcting them.

It takes personal awareness, sometimes professional help, and most of all determination and self-discipline to improve your speech—but it can be done. Demosthenes, the ancient Greek, was born with a slight speech impediment that made it difficult for him to articulate some words and project his voice loud enough to be heard by the multitude of his disciples. He didn't assume that failing to be incorrectable. Legend has it that he learned to surmount this handicap by placing several pebbles in his mouth when alone in the field and shouting so that his voice could carry hundreds of feet away. In time, his persistence paid off, and as every schoolchild knows, he became the greatest orator in all recorded history.

There are career counselors who suggest that the job seeker who is aware of his limitations in speech (whatever they may be) go back to school and enroll in an extended program of speech improvement. That's all well and good if you can afford to take time off your busy job hunt schedule and put everything aside, making this your priority. If it's not practical to pursue this course of action, you may wish to consider the following alternatives:

1. Make it a practice to devote some time during evenings and weekends to reading aloud—to a member of the family, a friend who may have been (or is) a speech major, or perhaps someone among your circle of acquaintances known to be an accomplished public speaker. Whoever that may be, ask him to point out noticeable (but correctable) faults in your speech pattern and diction— with no holds barred. To make this critique more realistic and more valuable, supply him with a list of questions the interviewer is likely to ask—he to assume the role of interviewer; you, the role of job applicant. Tape this question-answer scenario for subsequent review.

It would be helpful too, if your ''interviewer'' were to improvise questions of his own to observe how and in what manner you respond to them extemporaneously. This role-playing experience can be made more meaningful with the aid of a video camera with instant playback. Most people in high office, from the President of the United States down, follow this procedure in preparation for press conferences, interviews, and other important public utterances.

2. When listening to a playback of your own speech, be on the lookout for dropped word endings, garbled sounds, and the frequency of uh's and um's that interfere with the flow of speech, as well as mispronunciations and shortcomings in voice projection.

3. When your favorite newscaster or talk show host is on the air, pay particular attention to his or her voice and diction. As a rule, well-known personalities on national networks are selected for superior voice quality (among other attributes). Though their speech may at times fall somewhat short of grammatical perfection, it is for the most part colloquially acceptable and easy to understand.

One of the best examples to follow for effective speech in all its ramifications is the general run of pulpit clergymen who have acquired this ability as an integral part of their seminary training. Irreverently put, it's not what they say, but how they say it that stirs souls. Well-timed dramatic hand gestures, changes in facial expression, modulations in voice from an angel's whisper to a thunderous blast— all make the congregation sit up (at least, wake up) and take notice.

4. Without letting it interfere with your continuing job-search activities, register for short-term workshops or professional seminars in speech improvement, such as those given by the Dale Carnegie organization, American Management Associations, the Sales Executive Club, or join any of the Toastmasters' Clubs in your neighborhood. Coaching courses in various aspects of speech improvement are offered by local ''Y''s and adult education centers, many of them given after business hours.

With all the help you can get professionally or otherwise, bear in mind that you can't hope to magically change deeply ingrained speech habits overnight. What you can hope for realistically is to sharpen your awareness of your speech shortcomings, whatever they may be, and work on those that can be corrected or modified. It is not easy to entirely eradicate a strong regional accent. This is apparent to anyone as soon as the speaker opens his mouth, even if it's just to say "hello." It does not take the trained ear of a Professor Higgins to detect speech patterns of anyone raised in the deep South, the Boston area, the western states, or New York City and its environs.

It is difficult, or some say impossible, to get rid of a foreign intonation (characteristic of anyone who came to this country as a teenager or older). No coaching will do it, no matter how intensive or length of duration. A good example: the distinct gutteral voice and unmistakeably foreign intonation so evident in Henry Kissinger's speech pattern. But bear this in mind: though Kissinger and other outstanding personalities in public or political life may sound "different," they are, by and large, highly articulate speakers because they have learned to speak with ease, fluency, and grammatical correctness.

6

WORDS, PHRASES, AND EXPRESSIONS THAT DO YOU IN

W HEN INTERVIEWED FOR a job, be mindful of some of the more common errors in speech and vocabulary that are the marks of a person with limited education or someone just neglectful of how he comes across in conversation.

Here is a sampling of words, phrases, and expressions (misused, used too often, or grammatically incorrect) that give a job candidate a bad mark. See how many of these you find sneaking from time to time into your daily speech.

I seen this happen: The correct expression is, "I *saw* this happen," or, "I *have seen* this happen."

Less and less people: Incorrect. The correct phrase is "*fewer and fewer* people." The word *less* applies to quantity; *few* applies to number.

No one in their right mind: The phrase should be, "No one in *his* right mind." Presumably everyone has a mind of his own.

Confidentially, just between you and I and the lamppost: The correct pronoun is *me*, and you don't need the lamppost to lean on for emphasis.

This job is different than the others: The correct expression is, "This job is different *from* the others." When used in the comparative sense, the word *different* is always followed by *from*, not *than*.

I feel badly about this: The correct phrase is, "I feel *bad* about this."

Like I was saying: The correct phrase is, "*As* I was saying."

It's not what you know, but who you know that counts: Wrong. It's "*whom* you know that counts."

I will arrive at about 9 o'clock: This is incorrect. Use *at* or *about*, but not both.

I believe everybody should do their job well: The word *everybody* takes the singular. The correct phrase is, "everybody should do *his* (or *her*) job well."

Reoccur: It's more meaningful to say *occur again* or *recur*.

Can't hardly: This is a double negative and shouldn't be used. *Can hardly* is correct.

Heighth: There is no such word in the dictionary. The word is *height* (rhymes with bite).

Adapt, adopt: These two words are sometimes erroneously interchanged. To *adapt* is to adjust to a new condition or situation; to *adopt* means to take up and use an idea or practice as one's own, or to choose and follow a course of action.

Affect, effect: The word *affect* is a verb meaning to modify or influence, as in the sentence, "The loss of his job *affected* his self-esteem." *Effect* may be a verb or a noun. As a verb, it means to accomplish or bring about; as a noun, it means outcome or result. As examples: "His dominant personality has a marked *effect* on the staff"; "I believe I can *effect* a change for the better."

Can, may: Don't use *can* when you mean *may*. *Can* denotes ability; *may* denotes permission.

Biannual, biennial: *Biannual* (or semi-annual) means twice a year; *biennial* means once every two years.

Lie, lay: These words are often erroneously interchanged. You *lie* down to sleep, but you *lay* down a book.

Anywheres: The correct word is *anywhere* with no *s* at the end. This also applies to the word *nowhere*.

He don't know nothing: A double negative. The correct phrase is, "He *doesn't* know *anything*."

Of the several jobs I've held so far, none are as challenging as this one: Say, "none *is*." *None* always takes a singular verb.

Data: This is a peculiar word. *Data* is the plural for *datum*, yet is almost always used in the singular sense as, "This *data was* compiled by an eminent researcher."

Farther, further: *Farther* implies distance: *further* implies quantity or degree. "You walk *farther*; you hear nothing *further*."

Between, among: The following sentence will illustrate how these two words differ. "According to the will of the deceased, the estate is to be equally divided *between* you and me, leading other members of the family to quarrel *among* themselves."

Debits, credits: It seems strange there are people who are still fuzzy about the difference in meaning between *debits* and *credits*. Some years ago my office hired a bookkeeper-trainee fresh from a two-year business school. She apparently never got to comprehend the distinction between debits (accounts payable) and credits (accounts receivable). On a slip of paper tucked away in one corner of her desk drawer she wrote the following as a constant reminder to herself: "Debits means we own them; credits means they own us." Evidently she also wasn't aware of the difference between *owe* and *own* either. When she finally learned to tell the difference between debits and credits (and owe and own) she quit to get a better-paying job elsewhere. Who knows, perhaps to become head bookkeeper or financial advisor to a large corporation.

This here: The word *here* is an unnecessary hanger-on and sounds illiterate. *This* is sufficient.

I want to ax you: If you mean to inquire (not to cut down), the proper pronunciation is *ask*, not *ax*.

This ain't so: *Ain't* is the wrong contraction for *is not, am not,* or *have not*. The word *ain't*, however, is so commonly used, even by educated folk, that it is on the verge of being accepted in colloquial speech. But not yet. Elite grammarians still refuse to make that concession. For the time being, don't use *ain't* except for humorous effect, as Al Jolson employed it in, "You ain't heard nothin' yet."

Spoonfuls: Looks incorrect, doesn't it? But that's the way it is spelled and pronounced. *Spoonsful* is wrong.

Et cetera: Often mispronounced *ex cetera*. The word is rarely used in speech; it is reserved more for the written form where it is abbreviated *etc*.

Irregardless: A common redundancy. The proper word is *regardless*.

A new innovation: A redundancy. The word *innovation* implies something newly developed or introduced. Presumably every innovation is new.

Past history: All history is past.

Basic fundamentals: You can omit the word *basic*. All fundamentals are considered to be basic.

Old adage: Adage implies old. The dictionary defines *adage* as an old (usually wise) saying which has been popularly accepted as the truth.

True facts: All facts are presumed to be true—and that's a fact.

Estimated at about: *About* is not needed. An estimate is in itself an approximation.

#1 priority: Priority implies first rank in importance. To quote New York City's Mayor Koch, who facetiously remarked in a TV interview: "My first #1 priority is to reduce crime in the city streets. I have six other #1 priorities."

My personal friend: In most cases, *my friend* is enough. Have you ever heard of an impersonal friend?

Uniquely different: If it's unique, it's different. *Unique* means highly unusual, having no likeness or equal.

Advance planning: The word *advance* is superfluous. You generally plan before, not after.

A good recommendation: Is the opposite of a good recommendation a no-good (or bad) recommendation?

Consensus of opinion: This phrase is used loosely even by educated people who should know better. It's wrong. *Consensus* means a general agreement held by all or most people. It's sufficient to say *consensus is*. Consensus implies opinion.

Slurred pronunciations to look out for:
    F'instance, when you mean *for instance*
    Gonna, when you mean *going to*
    Wanna, when you mean *want to*
    Didja, when you mean *did you*
    In'ernational, when you mean *international*
    In'eresting, when you mean *interesting*
    Ledder, when you mean *letter*
    Should'na, when you mean *should not have*

Controversial: Some people pronounce it con-tro-ver-si-al, which is one syllable too many. The correct pronunciation is *con-tro-ver-shal*.

Incidentally: Pronounce it as *in-si-dent-lee*, not *in-si-den-tahl-lee* (which is one syllable too many.)

Accidentally: Here all five syllables are pronounced, *ak-si-den-tahl-lee*, not *ak-si-dent-lee*.

Li'bary: A lazy and wrong way of saying *library*. You should have outgrown that faulty pronunciation long before you finished junior high.

Due to the fact that: This is a roundabout way of saying *because*. In nearly all instances *because* conveys the intended meaning.

For the purpose of: A roundabout way of saying *to* or *for*.

In the event that: If is shorter and means the same thing.

Notwithstanding the fact that: A wordy way of saying *although* or *even though*.

Each and every one of you: This is a speechmaker's favorite cliche—a time-stretcher. Say, *each of you* or *every one of you*, but not both.

Long time no see: A glib colloquial for, *I haven't seen you for a long time*. Avoid it.

Per se: There is nothing wrong with this expression, per se. It is Latin for *in itself* or *by itself*. *Per se* is a favorite among freshly minted liberal arts graduates. In ordinary conversation it smacks of a literary affectation. Prescription: don't use *per se* more than once a day.

Hopefully: This word means *it is to be hoped*. It's a nice sounding word except it's been used too frequently. Count how many times you find yourself using the word *hopefully* in spoken or written form, and cut it in half, at least.

En toto: A high-falluting way of saying *altogether*. Strictly for Latin students.

Uptight: There's nothing intrinsically wrong with the word or the spelling. *Uptight* has gotten to mean edgy, overanxious, or tense. It is a buzzword with psychological overtones and should be put back on the couch.

Productionwise, Timewise, Profitwise, Economywise: All are buzzwords in the executive language.

Prioritorize: A buzzword which in plain English means *give priority to*.

Affordable: A favorite buzzword used by writers of advertising copy, implying that the product is well within the means of the purchaser. Since we normally don't speak the language of the professional copywriter, use it sparingly (if at all) in normal conversation.

Guesstimate: A coined expression meaning a *rough estimate*. It is a ligature of two words, *guess* and *estimate*. *Guesstimate* may have been popular a generation ago; it no longer is.

The statement was intentionally obfuscated: More people will understand you if you say, ''This statement was intentionally *confusing*.'' *Obfuscated* sounds like a dirty word.

I don't want to repeat again what I said before: There are too many negatives here to make it clear what the speaker means.

Include me out: A ''Goldwynism'' intended to mean *count me out* or *don't include me*.

Who is it? It's I: According to strict rules of grammar, *I* is correct, but *me* is what is generally used in this instance and is acceptable.

To tell you the honest truth: Stay away from this avowal of honesty. It signifies that the speaker has two kinds of truths to tell, honest and otherwise.

I know you're not kidding, but I'd like to ask you a question; ''Are you kidding?'': This is an example of words strung together that defy analysis. Here is another: ''I often sometimes do this.''

Know what I mean?: This expression repeated frequently in conversation indicates that the speaker is not exactly clear in his own mind what he means, but he hopes the listener is. Know what I mean . . . ?

Note: For an expanded list of misused words, malapropisms, tired cliches, fractured grammar, and common mispronunciations, read *A Modern Guide to English Usage* by Theodore M. Bernstein. This highly authoritative book will alert you to faults that you may not be aware of in your own speech. Another good book on the subject is *Strictly Speaking*, by the erudite TV personality and language critic Edwin Newman. You'll find it not only instructive but entertaining as well.

INTERVIEWS COME IN ALL
SIZES AND SHAPES

T HE AUTHOR OF a recently published book on job procurement tells his readers, ''Interviews can be fun.'' That's a glib statement to make. It may have a nice ring to it but it just isn't so. Here you are in the presence of someone you never met before, who by virtue of his official authority can affect your career one way or another in a scant 30 minutes or less. Admittedly, interviewing gets easier with practice as you become more aware of the criteria by which you are judged and learn to present yourself with greater self-assurance and conviction. Even at best, who can say that the average job applicant doesn't experience some degree of uneasiness every time he's interviewed.

There are different types of interviews, none of which are entirely free of tension. They come in all sizes and shapes, depending upon the nature of the job and corporate policy in staffing.

THE SCREENING INTERVIEW

The purpose of the screening interview is essentially to weed out those applicants who obviously fall short of meeting the basic requirements needed for

50

the job on hand. Screening reduces the many who apply to a manageable few who seem likely prospects worthy of further consideration in subsequent interview sessions.

In a large organization, screening as well as follow-up interviews are conducted by professionals trained in personnel work, whereas in a small company it may be a shirt-sleeve supervisor or office manager who does the interviewing, and often as not, the boss himself.

The routine procedure in the screening interview consists in the main of a brief discussion touching on a candidate's work history and motivation. In some cases where specific skills are called for, as in typing, word processing, or the graphic arts, the interview may be extended to allow additional time for a related performance test. This first interview with an applicant hardly—if ever—results in a firm job offer. The hiring decision is left for subsequent interview sessions which are usually of longer duration and conducted somewhat more informally.

The person assigned to a screening interview at this stage of the proceedings is not so much concerned with delving into the subtleties of the candidate's personality or an in-depth evaluation of his character as with his general image and deportment, and of course, with concrete evidence of work experience and educational background as revealed in the brief discussion or more fully stated in his resume and application form.

The interviewer must ever be alert not to allow a dud to slip through his fingers. This would be a serious reflection on his professional acumen. Indeed, repeated misjudgments in this respect may lead to his dismissal. More importantly, it could prove to be a costly mistake for the company he represents. It's been estimated that in large corporate enterprises, the recruitment, training, and breaking-in a top executive may run as high as $30,000; for those in middle management up to $15,000; and in the neighborhood of $3000 to $5000 for those below that rank.

THE SELECTION INTERVIEW

This is an intermediate stage between the Screening and the Hiring Interview for candidates who have successfully passed the first hurdle. For high-income positions any number of such interview sessions may be scheduled before the final Hiring Interview.

The motivation behind the Selection Interview is to probe deeper into the candidate's holistic background and experience—his salary progression in the companies he worked for, evidence of growth of responsibility and actual achievements, potentials, etc. Also at this time a closer view is taken of his personal attributes and that ephemeral ingredient called "style." Summing it all up, is the candidate the type of person who fits the corporate image?

As a rule, in the Selection Interview the relationship between interviewer and interviewee is somewhat less formal than is characteristic of a Screening Interview. Questions are generally broader in scope, more reflective in nature, and are inclined to be open-ended in phrasing to encourage the candidate to talk freely about himself. An open-ended question may run something like this: "How would you describe yourself?" or, phrased differently, "Tell me about yourself." In counter-distinction to this approach, direct questions evolve around specific points of information intended to elicit short factual answers. Direct questions are quite often preceded by "what," "who," "where," and "when." For example, "What was your top salary in your last job?," "Who recommended you to our company?," "Where did you get your training?," "When can you start, if the job is yours?" (An extended list of typical questions, both open-ended and direct appear in Chapter 8.)

THE HIRING INTERVIEW

The object here is to determine whether to extend a firm job offer to a candidate who meets, or comes close to meeting, the qualifications the company is looking for in a prospective employee. During this phase of the interview proceedings an attempt is made to finalize major points heretofore discussed involving responsibilities of the position as well as the degree of authority and chain-of-command that goes with it. Also included are such practical matters as starting salary, bonuses, insurance coverage, company policy regarding vested pensions, training programs and tuition reimbursement, and periodic salary and promotion reviews. Incidentally, this is a fortuitous time for the candidate to bring up the issue of a contract or letter of confirmation incorporating all matters agreed upon. For major jobs on the executive level, it may take a series of such sessions extending over a number of weeks before all issues are resolved to the satisfaction of the candidate and prospective employer.

INTERVIEW TECHNIQUES

Interviews can vary from cordial to brusk, or deliberately hostile, depending upon the nature of the job and (not to be discounted) the personality of the one conducting the interview.

The Stress Interview

This is the "bête noire" of interview techniques that a candidate most dreads. Instead of being made comfortable and at ease, here the candidate is placed in an awkward if not defensive position by the interviewer's hostile attitude and line of questioning. This is a deliberate tactic to observe at first hand the candidate's reaction to certain adverse conditions he's likely to encounter in sales, customer service, management, and other interpersonal on-the-job situations. With this in mind, the interviewer is not averse to resorting to sarcasm and on occasion to challenge the candidate's motives and integrity. Questioning may be preceded by such phrases as, "You mean to tell me . . . ?," "You claim that . . . ?," "How do you reconcile that with . . . ?" Or he may try a different tack entirely with questions like, "Why do you pull your earlobe whenever I ask for an explanation?" or "Do

you always wear a toupee?''

If you as a candidate find yourself in the hot seat, don't look upon the interviewer as an inquisitor or direct descendant of the Marquis de Sade. He may be a pussycat dressed in tiger's clothing, doing what he has to do. After clawing you at the beginning of the interview, don't be surprised if he returns to his normal character and shows himself to be a person who is understanding and considerate.

The Lunch Interview

This type of interview can take place away from the austere surroundings of a typical business office and be shifted to a comparatively quiet section of the company cafeteria. For the aspirant of a key position, however, a more congenial setting for a lunch interview is a better-than-average restaurant off grounds. There, over cocktails and a well-served lunch, he is accorded the social amenities of an invited guest with the interviewer acting as his host.

In this relaxed atmosphere, he will feel free to expound more fully about his long-range career plans, go into details about his professional history and achievements and (unguardedly) touch upon certain aspects of his private life and observations as well. But here a danger lurks! He may be inclined to disclose off-the-cuff tidbits about his previous employer's extramarital peccadillos or his own impending divorce, his off-center political views, or his emotional hangups. The interviewer-host begins to look like someone akin to a bosom friend or an erstwhile confidant. Unknowingly, the candidate can fall into a trap artfully set by his "friendly" host. If he's smart, he'll not lose sight of the fact that a job interview is strictly a business meeting no matter when or where it is held, or how it is conducted. His actions, words, deportment, and eating habits—every move he makes—will be carefully studied and taken note of. If he spends an inordinate amount of time selecting an item on the menu, it serves as a sign of indecision—a characteristic likely to show up on the job as well. Should he make use of the saltcellar and sprinkle salt over his yet untasted food, that also can have significance to his discerning host. It serves as a clue that the candidate is not one to evaluate a situation before applying a remedy. If his soup is tepid by the time it reaches the table and he accepts it complacently without calling the matter to the attention of the waiter, it could suggest that he lacks assertiveness—a negative trait that does not sit well for anyone aspiring to a position of authority. If truth be told, it is conceivable that the "tepid soup test" was arranged by the host in collusion with the maître d' to observe the candidate's reaction. Another Machiavellian trick (although rare) is to have the candidate's drink spiked with a double shot while the host's "cocktail" is nothing more than tonic water with an olive afloat. Somebody's head has to be clear in games people play!

With all the pitfalls confronting a job candidate in a lunch interview, there are compensating benefits to balance the scale. First, it serves to establish a closer rapport between the candidate and his prospective employer. Then too, it gives the candidate the opportunity to learn far more about the company and its inner workings than can be gleaned from the best annual reports or well-worded public relations utterances.

Lunch Hints

- You, as a candidate need not order exactly what your host does, but neither should you arbitrarily select the most expensive nor the lowest-priced items on the menu.

- To keep your breath fresh, bypass highly spiced dishes.

- Don't order finger-licking food such as fried chicken, lobster tail, or similar items which are messy to eat.

- Refrain from having more than one cocktail. Decline with thanks even if your host sets the example with a second.

- When lunch is over, don't insist on paying the tab or even the tip. You can safely assume that your host's expense account covers such business-related expenditures.

- Thank your host for the time he's taken off his busy schedule to meet with you, and for his hospitality. When you get home, follow up with a billet-doux to the same effect.

The Panel or Committee Interview

Here a candidate may find himself facing a number of functionaries of an organization acting jointly as an interview committee. This technique has long been employed by the Board of Education of New York City and other major school systems for interviewing prospective teachers. The committee as a rule is headed by a member of the Board of Examiners aided by a school principal and a department chairman in a specific subject area. It may also include a member of the PTA and at times a well-known figure in local community affairs.

The interview procedure followed here can take this course: Prior to the actual interview, the candidate is handed a typewritten sheet on which a typical classroom problem is described. He is then given 20 minutes or so to read and analyze the problem, after which he is called in to meet the committee. A typical problem may be worded something like the following:

"A student in your class has of late become so disruptive as to impede the learning progress of the rest of the class and openly challenges your authority. Discuss the steps you would take in such a situation."

The object here is to test the candidate's comprehension, his knowledge of fundamental principles of education, and his ability to apply them to a particular classroom situation. The committee is also interested in an evaluation of the candidate's general appearance, tact, decorum, and speech pattern.

The procedure followed in the private sector is somewhat similar. When a candidate is considered for an important position in sales or merchandising, for example, the panel of interviewers may consist of a V.P. in charge of personnel, a district manager in sales or merchandising, and, if the position involves policy-making and interfacing with other departments, possibly an industrial psychologist as well. The candidate may be presented a corporate problem in order to observe his manner of approach, his degree of reasoning ability, and, of course, his knowledge of the subject. A likely problem may be:

"Sales in our home-maintenance division have dipped 30% since last year when our closest competitor, Stanley Bros. Home Improvement Corp., initiated a new point-of-purchase promotion campaign. How do you analyze the situation and what recommendations can you offer for our company to regain its previous lead in the field?"

Here, as well as in the former example, the candidate is not expected to come up with quick-fix solutions and pat answers. The ideal candidate is reflective in his approach to a problem, even assertive, but never dogmatic. He doesn't represent himself as a know-it-all.

Being interviewed by a committee can turn out to be a somewhat more tense experience for the candidate than the normal one-to-one interview. He stands in front of multiple mirrors and must come out just right in each of them.

The Group Interview

This is an informal, discussion-type interview to which a select number of front-runner candidates are invited as a group to note how each responds to a given job-oriented situation. After presenting a prepared subject agenda, the interviewer (alone or in conjunction with another member of the staff) starts the discussion going, then assumes the role of moderator. The group interviewer is designed primarily for candidates for key positions in administration, management, and liaison work with other departments or the general public. Individual interviews may follow before a final hiring decision is reached.

The object of a group interview is not so much to ferret out information about a candidate's history and technical background (credentials were reviewed in previous one-to-one interviews) but rather to create a climate to better observe his leadership potentials, reasoning power, and ability to express himself clearly and persuasively in group interaction among his peers.

Many companies develop some type of formalized fact sheet by which to evaluate the candidate's total qualifications for the job. One such example is shown on the following page, based on questions asked the candidate during an extended interview session.

Interview Via Videotape

Here job candidates selected by the employer on the basis of their credentials as stated in their resumes and/or letters of application are not initially interviewed by the employer directly, but by an outside service organization commissioned to conduct and record screening interviews on videotape.

Employers for the most part are happy with this arrangement since it drastically cuts the expenses normally entailed in hosting untried candidates whom they have not previously met in person and who may not come up to expectations for the job on hand. Moreover, the use of video cassettes makes it feasible to view prospective candidates at times convenient to the powers that be, and to play back the cassettes as often as they find it expedient to determine which of the job candidates are to be invited to an in-depth person-to-person interview on company premises.

The employer assumes all costs in the interviewing procedure. There is no charge to the job candidate.

XYZ COMPANY, INC.
APPLICANT EVALUATION FORM

Name of Applicant _____ Position applied for _____
Address _____ Phone _____

WORK HISTORY	Yes	Doubtful	No
Does the applicant have the type of work history needed for the position for which he is being considered?			
Does his work history reveal a capacity for self-criticism as well as criticism by his superiors?			
Does he have a sound estimation of his worth to our company?			
Is there a strong indication that he wants the job?			
Judging by his work history, has the candidate grown in effectiveness with each change of job?			
Does his work history show that he is persistant and aggressive?			
Does his work history show attitudes of cooperativeness and good will toward companies he has worked for in the past?			
Does his work history show leadership potential?			
Does he have a specific career goal and a plan to achieve it?			
Does his work history show that he has the capacity to plan and organize?			
Does his work history show that he has achieved a professional level commensurate with his capabilities?			
Does his work history show him to be innovative and progressive?			
Does his work history show a capacity to work steadily and systematically?			

	Yes	Doubtful	No
Do his work credentials appear to represent a true evaluation of the applicant?			

EDUCATIONAL BACKGROUND

	Yes	Doubtful	No
Has the applicant shown evidence that he has had the kind of scholastic background needed for the position for which he is being considered?			
Does his school record reveal a desirable level of achievement?			
Does his scholastic background indicate that he has taken leadership roles in extracurricular activities?			
Does the applicant have the ability to express himself well, verbally and in writing?			
Does he possess the motivation and potentials to make the most of our in-service training programs?			
As a student, what seems to have been his pattern of attendance and punctuality?			
Has the applicant selected the right schools in line with his future career he had envisioned for himself as a student?			

ECONOMIC AND FINANCIAL HISTORY

	Yes	Doubtful	No
Does the applicant's record show that he has been systematic and intelligent in planning his finances?			
Are his economic goals in line with the opportunities offered by our company?			
Does he appear to be a person financially prudent and not overreaching?			

	Yes	Doubtful	No
Does consideration of salary seem to be his prime objective?			

PERSONALITY

Does the applicant seem vitally eager to succeed?

Does he possess the ability to be self-analytical?

Does he appear to be well-adjusted emotionally?

Does he seem to be stable and dependable?

Is he the kind of person you would like to work with?

Does he seem to have a good attention span and the ability to listen?

Does he seem to relate well to people?

Does he have varied outside interests to broaden his scope?

Is he well-read?

Does he have a healthy inquisitive nature?

Is he cheerful and of an optimistic disposition?

Is he the kind of person likely to stay long with the company?

Is he well-mannered?

Is he cooperative and flexible?

Does he possess a good measure of poise?

Is he well groomed and of good appearance?

Is he inclined to be argumentative rather than persuasive?

Is he the kind of person likely to take calculated risks when required?

	Yes	Doubtful	No
Is he the kind of person who can inspire trust and loyalty in others?			
Does he show a propensity to adapt to unforeseen situations?			
Does he appear to be socially mature?			
Does he project an image of confidence and well-being?			
Is he a person likely to work harmoniously with the staff?			
Does he seem to have a happy home life?			
Does he show good reasoning ability?			

Total score

COMMENTS

_____

_____

_____

_____

Interviewed by: _____ Date of Interview _____

Scoring rules: 2 points for each *Yes*; 1 for each *Doubtful*: 0 for each *No*.

QUESTIONS LIKELY TO COME UP DURING A JOB INTERVIEW

POSSIBLE QUESTIONS BY THE INTERVIEWER

The number and kind of questions asked by the interviewer will vary widely with the position the candidate applies for and the responsibilities involved. The questions are also determined by whether it is a perfunctory screening interview or one intended to probe in depth the job candidate—his attitude, thinking ability, and outlook on life, in addition to his educational and work background.

The questions shown here are not meant to be in any prescribed sequence. In fact, there is no prescribed sequence. You will also note that some questions are direct, while others are open-ended, reflective in nature, and allow for personal opinion. Concentrate particularly on those which you believe are most applicable to you. With this in mind, how well would you answer them if you were sitting opposite the interviewer's desk right now?

Tell me about yourself.

How did you get into the line of work you are in now?

Allowing fantasy full sway, who would you like to be, in either contemporary society or going back in history?

How did you handle the toughest decision you ever had to make, personally or on the job?

What has been your biggest disappointment?

A simplistic question; "Are you smart?"

If you were starting life all over again, what career or business would you consider in view of today's opportunities?

As a department manager, how would you go about establishing a good rapport with your staff?

Do you have any friends or relatives working for our company at the present time or in the past?

What do you consider to be your major strengths; what do you concede to be your major weaknesses?

How do you react to criticism by superiors, if in your judgment the criticism is unwarranted?

From your resume and our conversation so far, I see that you've had many short-duration jobs. Why?

Are you sure this is the kind of work you'd be happy doing?

Your resume states that you were employed in Civil Service for more than 10 years. What made you leave to enter the private sector?

What's the nicest thing you've ever done in your life of which you are justifiably proud? What, if anything, have you done that you regret bitterly?

What was your salary progression in the last two jobs you've held?

Here are 10 criteria for evaluating a job offer. In what order of priority would you list them? Take time to consider.

a) job security

f) geographic location of company

b) challenge

g) type of people you work with

c) salary and fringes

h) opportunity for innovation

d) reputation of company

i) feelings of power and authority

e) opportunity to reach the top

j) chance to be your own boss

Have you ever been turned down for a salary increase? If so, what reason were you given and what did you do about it?

Do you have any outstanding debts and how do you expect to clear them?

We never underestimate our competition. Can you name three of our leading competitors and point out some unique advantages they may have over our company?

About your financial status: Do you have any outside income? Approximately how much does it amount to? From what source is it derived?

In what specific ways will our company benefit by hiring you?

How did you learn about this job opening?

I have your resume in front of me, but can you tell me personally about what you believe to be your special qualifications for this job—scholastically, technically, and otherwise?

How well acquainted are you with our company and its corporate structure?

In your considered opinion, what makes our company "special" compared to others in the field?

Would you recommend your last place of employment to others?

How do you explain the rather long gaps in your employment history?

How was your education financed throughout your college years?

Do you have any fear of flying that may deter you from traveling by air?

How did you get your first job?

How much time do you spend with your family?

What is the model and year of the car you own?

Do you own your own home or do you rent?

Are you taking any day or evening courses at the present time? Are you planning to do so in the future?

In a recent questionnaire distributed among students in a theological seminary, one of the questions asked was, "What career would you have pursued, if not the clergy?" Of the seminarians polled, 87% stated "a career on the stage." What would be *your* alternate career choice if you were not in your present line of work?

Do you prefer working as a member of a team or would you rather work alone?

What would you do if this were the last day on earth?

What are your career goals for the foreseeable future? Have they shifted recently? If so, why?

How has your education and training prepared you for this job?

If you have introduced any innovations in your last few jobs, how did they work out? Have your efforts been acknowledged and duly rewarded?

What salary are you looking for?

It's been said, "A good supervisor is one who has made himself useless." What's your thinking about this?

When was your last medical checkup and what were the findings?

Do you have any references we can follow up to verify your credentials? Who are they and is it okay to contact them?

Do you have any physical or emotional handicaps which could possibly hamper your performance and growth on the job?

A three-prong question: You tell me you've moved about widely throughout the United States and abroad.
    (a) Why? (b) What did you gain by it? (c) Do you feel you can settle down now?

How do you usually spend your after-working hours and weekends?

Everyone has some favorite hobbies. What are yours?

Who in the business world has served as your source of inspiration? In what ways has this guided you?

How good is your memory? Early in our conversation I mentioned the name of the founder of the company. Do you remember it?

What other companies are you prospecting at the present time?

From my own experience I know that not all subjects in the school curriculum are worthwhile. However, we all had our favorites. What was your favorite subject and who was your most unforgettable teacher?

If you won a million-dollar sweepstakes, how would you spend it?

Can you convince me that you are right for the job?

It's been said that the only way to get a worker to do his best is to get out of his way. How do you feel about that?

How have you spent your time during the long gaps between jobs?

You say your goal is to reach regional manager level within three years. How do you expect to achieve that?

In your opinion, what attributes make for the ideal supervisor or boss?

Would you be willing to submit to a lie detector test if the nature of the job made that advisable or mandatory?

What, if any, editorial contributions have you made to publications in your field?

As you view it, what makes for a happy marriage?

Would you be in a position to work overtime, if required?

Did you ever walk out on a job without giving due notice? If that be the case, what were the circumstances that led to such an action?

Name three books you've read in the last half year or so.

What trade or professional journals do you subscribe to?

Speaking self-analytically, would you say you have a competitive nature? If so, how did this quality manifest itself in the jobs you've held? Where did it get you?

What's your idea of success?

In school, what extracurricular activities did you participate in? Which ones did you excel in to reach leadership level?

How do you feel about your family?

What were the biggest pressures on your last job?

All things considered, are you confident you can handle this job?

How often and in what way did you communicate with your staff or superiors?

What new skills or capabilities have you developed in the past year?

Would you say you've achieved a measure of happiness in all life has to offer?

As you know, we have branches in other large cities and in some of the world's capitals. Do you have any preference for a specific job location?

What foreign languages do you speak or write with a fair degree of proficiency?

If hired, how long do you plan to stay with us?

Do you have any mixed emotions about working in a department headed by a female executive?

In a TV interview, Egypt's martyred President Sadat is quoted as saying, "I would like them to write on my tombstone the following: 'He has lived for peace and has died for principles.'" What epitaph would *you* want to have inscribed on your tombstone?

What type of people do you have no patience for?

To what extent do you require liquor or other stimulants to cope with tension?

Describe the steps you would take before dismissing someone in your department who has been sloughing off for a long time?

What plan of action do you take when facing a tough problem?

Do you have any difficulty making a decision? And once having made it, do you stick to it, regardless?

If you've been absent from your job from time to time, what were the circumstances of this less-than-perfect attendance?

What do you envision for yourself, two, three, and five years from now?

How is it that a person with your accomplishments is out of work, and has been so, for the past ten months?

What section of the newspaper do you turn to first?

What's your favorite TV program, and why?

What are some of the professional seminars and trade conferences you've attended in the last twelve months? What have you gained thereby and who paid for your attendance?

What distance do you live from our company's location? What means of transportation would you use to come to work?

To what extent are you financially solvent not to have to be overly concerned about money matters?

Looking back, what mistakes do you regret making that you might have averted had you exercised greater foresight?

To use a colloquial expression, tell me "Who is the boss in your family?"

Are you a traditionalist in terms of company-prescribed code of dress, or do you look upon such as an unnecessary bureaucratic imposition restricting individual choice and liberty?

What great things would you attempt if you knew you could not fail?

Can you name the two United States Senators of your state?

Do you have the guts when necessary to take issue with your superior or a member of your department in presenting an opposing point of view?

In what ways are you innovative? Can you illustrate with some specific examples?

How often do you volunteer to head a committee or a special task force?

What does it take for you to lose your temper?

Why do you want to switch careers at this stage of your professional life?

What do you think makes you unique, and how can this quality be utilized by our company?

Would you consider yourself a confirmed teetotaler, or do you imbibe in the proper social milieu?

After you completed your formal education, did your career goals change? If so, what direction did they take?

To what extent, if any, have you contributed to the support of your family, or assisted in meeting the educational expenses of brothers and sisters?

Do you follow an organized plan for savings and expenditures?

Did any previous employer ever refuse to give you a reference? If so, why?

What experience have you had in supervising people whose technical know-how exceeded yours?

What is your off-the-cuff impression of the company you worked for last?

Do you make it a practice to meet socially with the families of your associates and coworkers?

In your last job did members of your staff feel free to come to you with personal problems not necessarily related to the job?

As a department head, were you known to run a tight ship—allow no corner cutting and go strictly by the book?

Did you feel that your subordinates had a personal affection for you? In what way did they show it?

As a person about to reenter the labor market after a lapse of some years, what have you done to upgrade your skills to prepare for this position?

I am impressed with your long and distinguished career in the armed services. Will you tell me how our company can benefit by employing you, when apparently the functions of this job seem to have little or no relevance to your past military duties?

If your husband/wife is employed, do your careers mesh, or do they tend to conflict?

Have you ever been honored at a testimonial affair or been the recipient of an award or citation?

You tell me that you are divorced. What contributed to the breakup of your marriage and what have you learned from your experience?

Your salary progression on your last job shows that you were evidently well appreciated by the company. Why aren't you working there any more?

Have you ever been refused bond? If so, will you please explain the circumstances?

As a supervisor, would it bother you to fire an employee with due reason? What, for example, might some of the reasons be for such a course of action?

What major trends do you foresee for our industry in the next three to five years?

Why are you planning to leave your present job?

How do you feel about your readiness to function in a more responsible position than you've ever held before?

We are not able to meet the salary you ask for. How far can you lower your sights to be more within range of the company salary structure for your type of position?

It's been said, ''A man is a failure if he does not benefit by his disappointments.'' How does this relate to your life and career?

Do you consider yourself an able public speaker with sufficient confidence and experience to address trade groups and business functions?

We all have our biases and hangups. What are some of yours?

Do you believe in astrology, and if so, to what extent are you guided by your personal horoscope?

As a recent graduate with limited on-the-job work experience, in what ways can you prove to be an asset to our company?

It's been said, ''The only way to get anything done right is to do it yourself.'' Will you please comment on that?

Why do your friends like you and why do those who are not your friends dislike you?

Did you ever sustain a serious injury while on the job? If so, tell me about it.

When can you start after you've been notified that you've been given the job?

Does your present employer know that you are planning a job change?

How do you manage to keep interview dates while still employed on a full-time job?

I've asked many questions. Is there anything you'd like to ask *me* before we terminate the interview?

In addition to your responses to anticipated questions, be mentally prepared to handle gnawing personal problems that may surface during the course of the interview; such as: being a former alcoholic, being subject to epileptic fits, separation from the army on a dishonorable discharge, a history of drug addiction, being considerably older than the average applicant for the job.

Assuredly, no knowledgeable interviewer will go on record asking the applicant point blank questions which can be interpreted as being discriminatory in nature. Nonetheless, in an extended discussion, some personal situations may be tangentially touched upon. It is your right to decline answering any question which you feel impinges on your private life and is entirely irrelevant to your performance on the job. If you exercise that right, do so tactfully and without rancor. At all times guard against getting into a heated confrontation with the person interviewing you.

POSSIBLE QUESTIONS BY THE JOB APPLICANT

Don't hesitate to bring up any questions relating to the particulars of the job not previously covered or sufficiently gone into. No interviewer will hold that against you. Quite the contrary; his image of you could very well be enhanced thereby. It demonstrates an active interest in the job applied for and all that it entails.

A good opening question could be, "Mr. _____, what are you looking for in a prospective employee to fill this position?" The others shown here may follow any order that seems feasible under the circumstances.

Can you tell me what happened to my predecessor?

As department head, how many people will be under my direct supervision, and how long have they been with the company?

Are other applicants being considered for this position?

Who will be my in-line superior if I am hired?

Who in the company has the final say in the hiring decision?

What would a person with my qualifications have to look forward to in terms of mobility within the company?

To what extent does this job entail overtime, extensive travel, or possible relocation?

Is the company part of a conglomerate, or does it plan to be so in the near future? If so, how will this affect me?

Am I expected to join a trade or company union to work here?

Could you arrange for me to get a letter of confirmation or a contract covering all matters agreed upon in our discussion?

Will it be feasible for me to take a brief guided tour to see your operational facilities and perhaps have an opportunity to meet some of the people I'd be working with?

Is this job seasonal or permanent?

Can you tell me something about the chain-of-command in the organizational structure of the company and how I fit into it?

How is promotion decided on here—by seniority, quality of performance, or on another basis?

Is there a company cafeteria or dining area on the premises for principals and staff?

Do you have on hand printed material covering company policy on such matters as insurance and pension plans, basis for promotion and periodic salary review, subsidized tuition, and other benefits and perks?

Does the company provide parking facilities for employees?

If hired, what time allowance would I have to clear my desk on my present job and help my boss to break in my replacement?

Would it be possible for me to obtain a copy of a recent newsletter or other company publication?

What salary package do you have in mind for this position?

Will there be subsequent interviews after this, before a hiring decision is made?

If for whatever reason I don't fit the role for this job, do you know of anyone who might be interested in a person with my qualifications? Could you perhaps arrange an interview for me?

Don't keep asking a barrage of questions, one after another, to an extent where the interviewer is annoyingly interrupted. For all you know he may take up the very topics you wanted to ask about during the course of the interview. If, however, you find the interview lagging or dotted with uncomfortable periods of silence, a few well-selected questions on your part could bring the interview back on the track and at the same time clear up certain facts important to your understanding of the job and how you fit into it.

THE BIONIC JOB APPLICANT
(A Fantasy)

WHAT ATTRIBUTES IN addition to know-how does the interviewer look for in the ideal job applicant?

Here is a partial bill of particulars:

The ideal job applicant is unobtrusively aggressive, tactful, innovative, co-operative, and reliable; someone who gets along with his superiors as well as with his subordinates; never loses his cool; has no psychological hangups; is blessed with a dynamic personality that matches Billy Graham's; has an impressive track record; someone with a sense of humor; is a polished speaker with a voice and diction that would have made Orson Welles take notice; someone who is able to compose and type committee reports with ease; is a good organizer; appreciates constructive criticism; is ever prompt in his appointments; someone with a well-structured career goal, yet is flexible; someone who is civic minded—a volunteer fund-raiser for the United Way, president of the PTA, and foster parent to one or two children in Guatemala; someone with a happy home life; someone who was an Eagle Scout at thirteen (a distinction that only a meager 2.5% of scouts ever achieve at any age).

In other words, the interviewer is on the lookout for a job applicant who is an exact copy of himself!

Is there more? Yes, "much, much more," as they say in the commercials.

He is also a good mixer; "fits" the organization; is a potential leader and self-starter; someone with a computer-like memory who never forgets a name; makes it a practice to always clear his desk before leaving the office (after everyone has clocked out for the day); has a "clean" look about him (whatever that means); is optimistic about the future; has the courage of his convictions; is not afraid to take calculated risks; and is a troubleshooter and problem solver par excellence. He is enthusiastic, smiling, and cheerful at all times. Of course, he is in great physical shape, with a posture like a West Point cadet; of fine appearance—always well dressed and immaculately groomed.

Sure, it won't be easy for you to measure up to all this, but see how close you can come.

As the Head of Personnel said to his new assistant, "Timothy, if a guy like this comes along, grab him! If it's a female, you will be careful, won't you?"

10

63 GUARANTEED WAYS
TO MUFF A JOB INTERVIEW

THE INTERVIEW IS the next to last stage of your entire job search campaign. The final stage, of course, is getting a firm job offer.

The "leads" you managed to get from obliging relatives and friends who wanted to help you out, or owed you a long-standing favor they were glad to redeem; the total stranger sitting next to you on that long plane ride from New York to Seattle who owed you nothing but liked the way you looked or talked, and to whom you handed a copy of your resume just in case he knew of someone; the weeks of preparation that went into researching the right companies; the out-of-pocket expenditures and the time entailed in printing and mailing stacks of resumes (with individually typed cover letters)—all these are not worth a tinker's damn if in the end you muff the interview.

Here's how to become an interview fatality!

1. Start off by telling the interviewer what a louse your last employer was, and how you got even with him by quitting at the height of the busy season.

2. Have a wad of gum in your mouth and keep chewing away. It's said that chewing helps tone up your facial muscles.

3. Nonchalantly light up a cigarette even though you see no ashtray around. The interviewer is *sure* to get one for you.·

4. Tell the interviewer what a great guy your psychiatrist is, the one you've been seeing two evenings and one afternoon a week for the past three years. You'll get an "A" for your attempt at self-improvement.

5. Give him a blow-by-blow description of your most recent divorce.

6. Say you would be curious to know what product or services the company is best known for.

7. Make it a practice to contradict the person interviewing you. The idea is to come out on top. To hell with the pap expounded by Dale Carnegie and Benjamin Franklin!

8. Languidly dangle one foot over the side of the armchair to indicate that you are as relaxed as when lounging in your own living room, watching the Late Show. Make yourself at home.

9. Arrive late to the interview. Explain why. Here are some suggestions that go over big:
   a) "This sure is a difficult place to get to!"
   b) "Try to get a cab in this rainy weather, especially at 4 o'clock in the afternoon."
   c) "That watch of mine never keeps correct time."
   d) "I could have sworn I had the right address."

10. If your quick mind races ahead of the interviewer's, finish his sentences for him before he finds the right words. You're sure to ingratiate yourself for coming to his aid.

11. From the very first, get things straightened out about salary, vacations, and fringe benefits as evidence of your primary interest in the job.

12. During the course of the interview, occasionally glance at your watch to hint you're in a bit of a hurry and have other things to take care of. If time seems to drag, give your watch a good shake.

13. Hand the interviewer one of your shopworn resumes that by now looks as ancient as the Dead Sea Scrolls.

14. Come to the interview minus a handkerchief when you have the sniffles. Ask the interviewer for a Kleenex. Then for another. He probably has some tucked away somewhere.

15. Insinuate that you know someone upstairs who's pulling for you. This leaves the interviewer with no alternative but to hire you on the spot.

16. Plunk down your bag or portfolio or anything else of the sort on his already cluttered desk.

17. Politely stifle a yawn when the interviewer continues to hold forth about his firm and the important role he plays in it.

18. If you're wearing a coat, keep it on during the course of the interview. This will serve as a cue that you don't expect to spend more time with him than necessary.

19. See how many times you can include *I*, *me*, or *mine* in your part of the conversation. Modesty is for second raters.

20. Go on the theory that if you speak low or mumble under your breath, the interviewer is likely to pay greater attention to what you are saying. A hang-down overgrown mustache, or resting your chin on your hand, also help.

21. Pass some derogatory remark about the receptionist you encountered in the outer office. He may have misjudged him/her all these years he/she has been with the company.

22. Follow Mel Brooks' advise: "Always tell the truth, whether it's true or not." Pinocchio's nose got longer and longer with each lie; yours probably won't.

23. When entering the office, brighten your expression with a smile, but only if something funny is going on. Most of the time stay expressionless. Everyone appreciates a sourpuss. There is entirely too much levity going on in this world!

24. When the interview seems to be going your way, linger a little longer. Keep on talking. Something may come up to turn the tide against you. Why stop when you are ahead?

25. Add a touch of glamor to your appearance. Show up to the interview with dark glasses, regardless of the season. Better still, wear the mirror-type where the interviewer can see a dual image of himself when looking at you.

26. When feasible, turn a discussion into a lively debate, with you gaining points. This will be especially appreciated in the presence of a secretary or anyone else who happens to be around.

27. Regard any incoming or outgoing phone calls during the interview as a personal intrusion. Sulk a little. Don't fail to conceal your annoyance.

28. If during the interview he takes it into his head for some strange reason to ask the same question twice, tell him you've answered it before.

29. When the interviewer lights up a cigarette and you are proud to be a non-smoker who recently kicked the habit, he'll be grateful if you deliver a short lecture on the harmful effects of smoking. Quote the Surgeon General to back you up.

30. When asked to explain the many short-duration jobs shown in your resume, answer that you believe in diversifying your experience. Staying with one company for any length of time is stultifying.

31. Should he wonder how you manage to keep interview appointments while holding down a 9-to-5 job, say that you called in sick. No doubt he will consider this little gambit a stroke of ingenuity.

32. Regard the person interviewing you as someone far beneath you in intelligence and experience—a zero flunky occupying the big chair. This private appraisal is bound to show in your face and general attitude.

33. When asked what your career objective is, you can say, "Well—for the time being, to land a job." When asked what it may be three to five years hence, a good reply (with philosophic overtones) is, "In this rapidly changing world who can look that far ahead?" "It's all in the stars," is a good answer, too.

34. It's good manners and protocol to always address a male interviewer as "Sir," regardless of whether he is older or younger than you. What if he squirms a little or becomes flustered at this unwanted token of respect? If it's a female interviewer, you'll pay her homage by addressing her either as "Madam" or "Ma'am."

35. Identify yourself as a reliable office fink. Relate to the interviewer how on your last job you were instrumental in getting the receptionist fired by reporting that on several occasions he/she took two-hour lunches. This type of information ingratiates you no end. Every company needs at least one spy-in-the-sky fink to keep the ship on an even course.

36. By all means, stick up for your constitutional rights by refusing to submit to a polygraph test, even if that is part of the screening procedure for that particular position. What do they take you for anyway, Billy Liar?

37. Tell the interviewer about some of those clever innovations you introduced on a previous job with a firm that subsequently went into bankruptcy. What if it puts a bug in his ear that there might have been a correlation between those innovations of yours and the resulting demise of the company?

38. Make it a point to be informed about the latest labor laws relating to affirmative action and equal opportunity regulations, and be sure to let the interviewer know that, at the outset. Be a freedom fighter! Show true grit!

39. Relate to the interviewer some of the goings-on in the company you previously worked for that you think he might want to know about, adding, "This was told to me in strictest confidence." This will undoubtedly impress him that you are a person of sterling character in whom trust can be placed.

40. Let the interviewer know that what most interests you in working for his company is its proximity to the local "Y," your temporary address until your interlocutory divorce comes through.

41. As testimony of your integrity, intersperse your conversation with "To be perfectly honest," "To tell you the truth," or "I'll level with you." This is very convincing because it lets the interviewer know that though you may not always tell the truth, this time you really are.

42. If you happen to be partial to loud colors, come decked out to the interview looking like an open beach umbrella, even if it's a funeral director's job you are applying for.

43. Appear at the interview accompanied by a pal of yours, making it a ménage à trois.

44. To show why you want the job, mention that your unemployment insurance is about to run out.

45. Sartorial note: Tidy up a bit *after* the interview to cancel out the imperfect initial image you may have projected in the actual interview.

46. Dress in some off-beat outfit no matter if you're interviewing for a high-level managerial position in banking, sales, or the like. Break the establishment dress code. Be a trend-setter, not a follower!

47. As a female, assume your male interviewer to be lecherous. Or, if you are male, assume your female interviewer to be wanton. Dress provocatively to catch his/her roving eye. Make the most of your natural endowments.

48. During the interview reminisce a little about your early childhood, whether the subject comes up or not. Mention the members of your family, their ages, and other vital statistics. Keep up this narrative till the interviewer begins to yawn openly. Don't fail to show him family photos and other sentimental memorabilia you carry in your wallet.

49. To *brace* yourself and be in good cheer, stop over at the Happy Hour Bar down the street for a snifter or two just before the interview. To *unbrace* yourself (should you find yourself too jumpy) take a couple of Valiums.

50. When offered a chair, politely decline by saying, "No, thank you, I'd rather stand." This elevated position gives you a strategic advantage because it forces the interviewer to look up at you.

51. Crack a few jokes. They needn't be germane to the discussion. Anyway, they will liven things up a bit and give the interviewer less time to probe what you are evidently trying to withhold. Heard any new ethnic jokes lately?

52. As the interviewer turns the pages of your portfolio, keep up a running commentary about each item. If by chance (or choice) he turns two or more pages at a time, call it to his attention immediately. No skipping, please!

53. Tell the interviewer why you quit or were dismissed from some of the jobs you've held. He'll probably be empathetic with the problems you've encountered with your previous employers.

54. Mention that your ultimate goal is to go into the same type of business as soon as you gain experience and save up sufficient capital. It shows the interviewer that you have initiative and are enterprising.

55. Your mother always nagged you about biting your fingernails. Why stop now? It gives you something to do during the interview.

56. Don't bother to stop over at the restroom before the interview. If the interview lasts longer than anticipated—oy vay, you shouldn't know from it!!

57. Continue to mispronounce the interviewer's name until he no longer bothers to correct you.

58. If the interviewer appears to have a sympathetic ear, why not confide in him as you would in a dear aunt/uncle or your favorite bartender? He has probably nothing more worthwhile to do than to listen to your personal problems.

59. Keep hammering away at what a hotshot you are in your field. Convey the impression that you can't imagine how the company managed to get by without you all these years.

60. When asked what your favorite leisure activities might be, say watching TV game shows and catching up on what's happening in the world as reported by the *National Enquirer*.

61. When shaking hands with the interviewer, extend the tips of your fingers, keeping the rest to yourself. Or overdo the handshake bit by vigorously pumping his hand up and down like the rickety handle of the village water pump.

62. To get an instant feedback, at the end of the interview session ask the interviewer sportingly, "How'd I do, coach?"

63. After you have succeeded in making a good sales pitch, don't ask for the job outright. Let the interviewer guess if you really want the job or not.

11

THE INTERVIEW—
PRELUDE TO A JOB OFFER

ONE OF YOUR many job-search techniques has finally paid off and your qualifications proved to be of sufficient interest to a prospective employer to want to meet you personally. This face-to-face meeting gives him (or whoever does the interviewing for the company) the opportunity to discuss your qualifications more fully in terms of the requirements of the job, and at the same time to observe you at close range with a view of coming up with a value judgment of you as a person and as a prospective employee.

As an applicant, in any job interview situation, you are bound to be tense no matter how relaxed the interviewer may try to make you feel in his attempt to have you reveal yourself fully. As sure as God made little green apples, he will take note of your knowledge of his company, the manner in which you respond to questions as well as in the kind of questions you ask him, and even how you talk, sit, smile, your enthusiasm (or lack of it) and, of course, your general appearance. Nothing you do or say is likely to pass him by. His impression of you will either be mentally fixed or, in some cases, qualitatively rated on an applicant evaluation form such as shown on page 56. The results of his observations will be the basis for determining whether you are rejected, placed in a doubtful category, be invited for subsequent interviews, or, in some unusual circumstances, offered the job forthright.

Interviewing is sometimes called an art. Some elevate it to a science. It is neither. Interviewing is a learned skill, as is proficiency in teaching, law, accountancy, or high-wire acrobatics. It may be that the person interviewing you is self-taught in interviewing techniques—someone who has acquired and sharpened his skill on the job. In large organizations the interviewer is likely as not a thoroughly trained professional with formal schooling in personnel management, human resources, or psychology, and may hold a B.A. or higher degree in his field of specialization. No matter how the interviewer has acquired his skill, he has learned how to size you up, how to get you to volunteer information (sometimes not to your advantage) through open-ended questioning, and how to read between the lines of your resume. He also knows how to read between the lines of what you say and *don't* say, and how to control the interview. At any rate, you can assume that a professional interviewer is fully prepared to meet you head on. How well prepared are *you*, the job candidate?

Of course, it is not expected that you possess the same kind of training to be a match for him. You are not a professional interviewer, nor are you (perish the thought!) a professional job seeker.

Most of us just don't acquire sufficient field experience in being interviewed to become proficient at it. However, what you should, and must, do is prepare yourself as well as you can—on your own if possible (or with professional help if need be)—to familiarize yourself thoroughly with what the interviewer looks for in a candidate likely to measure up to the requirements of the job. Unless you are well prepared, you may be handing over the job you always wanted—the one just within your grasp—to a competing candidate who is perhaps less technically qualified than you but has made a concerted effort to prepare himself for the interview proceedings. In short, you can easily lose out to someone who has done his homework—something you neglected to do.

All that precious time, effort, and expense involved to reach the interview stage of your entire job-search campaign can lead to disappointment and rejection if you fail in one way or other during those crucial 30 to 40 minutes when you meet the interviewer in person or in subsequent and longer interviews, if you are still in the running.

Study the job candidate's 11 cardinal rules of interviewing that is outlined and discussed in Chapter 13. If diligently adhered to, they give you an unbeatable advantage over your competitors for the same job. At all times, especially in a tight labor market when employers get choosy, you must make a conscientious effort to outperform the competition in all aspects—appearance, attitude, enthusiasm, tact, courtesy, and other such personal attributes. In general, the applicant who knows how to interview best gets the best job offers.

12

CHECKLIST OF THINGS TO DO FOR TOMORROW'S INTERVIEW

ASSUMING THAT YOU have diligently done your homework in the long-range preparation involved in an extended job search, here is a reminder of some last minute matters to take care of before setting out on that important interview date.

1. *Select and lay out your complete interview wardrobe, head to foot.*

Carefully go over what you plan to wear for the day: shirt or blouse, tie, suit, skirt, dress, shoes, hose, and other components (including accessories) mentioned in Chapter 4.

Are your shoes well-shined? Is your tie spotlessly clean? Is there a loose button that needs reinforcing? How about a freshly laundered handkerchief, small comb and mirror, make-up compact, and a packet of mints or other breath freshener?

2. *Sort out the credentials you plan to bring with you.*

Collectively, these most likely will include (in addition to several copies of your resume) letters of commendation, clips of published articles, printouts of your latest sales records, and other tangible evidence of achievements in your field. If you are in the performing arts or in advertising, you will naturally include carefully selected photos or actual examples of your professional work—all neatly arranged in a portfolio or attaché case. Be sure to avoid anything that looks shopworn or dated.

A word about personal calling cards: It's professional to have a personal calling card for interviewing. Have a few of them ready in your wallet to present to the receptionist and interviewer by way of introduction.

3. *See that you have on hand a pocket-size memo book for notes and two pens.*

Why two pens? Everybody has at one time or another had the exasperating experience when that never-fail pen unexpectedly runs dry or for whatever unknown reason plays dead so that no coaxing, pleading, or shaking will induce it to come back to life. (If pen #2 likewise refuses to cooperate, well then, it's just not your day!)

Item check of things to take along to an Interview ✓

• WALLET & CHANGE	
• POCKET HANDKERCHIEF	
• TOILET ITEMS: comb, brush, mirror, etc.	
• PRE-TESTED PEN	
• SMALL NOTEBOOK	
• COPY OF RESUME	
• PORTFOLIO OR FOLDER	
• PERSONAL BUSINESS CARDS	
• LIST OF QUESTIONS FOR INTERVIEWER	
• SELECTED CREDENTIALS	

As to a memo-book: You will find it will come in handy for listing previously formulated questions you plan to ask the interviewer, as well as for occasionally jotting down points of information covered during the course of the interview; most of all for the name, address, phone number of the company, date and time of interview, and (if known) name and title of the person who will interview you.

4. *Review notes and other data you compiled to help prepare you for the interview.*

These may be based on either extensive reading or things you have learned from past interviews which upon reflection you feel fell short in performance. The emphasis here is to see to it not to repeat those mistakes and indiscretions in the forthcoming interview.

If part of your preparation included a taped rehearsal interview, this is a good time to listen to it once more. If you've recorded it on videotape, so much the better, since it permits you to both listen and see yourself objectively in an interview situation—from the time you enter the office to the conclusion of the interview.

Next, go over the series of questions shown in Chapter 8, particularly those that apply to your situation, and verbally answer them as you would in the actual interview. Also review the questions that you've jotted down in your notebook—questions you plan to ask the interviewer.

5. *Provide yourself with sufficient cash for the anticipated expenditures of the day.*

You'll need coins for exact bus fares or other means of public transportation, money for cabs, pay phones, ''coffee 'n'' stopovers, or a more substantial lunch break during the day.

6. *Get a good night's rest.*

If, in anticipation of tomorrow's interview, you feel too edgy to fall asleep, do some physical exercise—jogging, pushups, or whatever—to help fatigue you sufficiently to fall soundly asleep. As an added measure, finish up with a warm bath and a glass of milk. The amino acid in the milk (said to serve as a natural tranquilizer) helps you to unwind and sleep better.

Caution: Refrain from taking sleep-inducing pills or more potent drugs. Either they will make you slumber sweetly beyond the time you intended to arise, undisturbed by the alarm clock buzz, or else you may experience a lingering drowsiness during next day's interview session, making you look and act as if you just emerged from the Recovery Room.

Last, synchronize your wristwatch with radio time.

13

11 CARDINAL RULES
FOR A SUCCESSFUL INTERVIEW

How you interact with your prospective employer determines in large measure how well you come out in the interview. You would be patently unfair to yourself if you venture forth to an interview without bearing in mind the 11 cardinal rules developed in this section. Take time to read them more than once and apply them the very next time you are invited to an interview.

Rule 1.   Show That You Are Knowledgeable About the Company and Its Operation

The assumption is that you've made a conscientious effort prior to the interview to research the company (its range of products and services, its problems and its prospects, its status in the industry), and, if possible, something about the interviewer himself.

This background will be of immeasurable help in directing your sales pitch and the strategy you pursue in your presentation. Interviewers are always favorably disposed towards applicants who not only know the field but have the foresight to learn all they can about the particular company they hope to be associated with.

To an enterprising job seeker, tracking down information about a company is not a difficult task. There are numerous trade directories available where you can find pertinent facts about any large firm of particular interest to you. Then, too, there are annual reports issued regularly by all public corporations, items of interest in the business sections of newspapers and other publications, trade gossip and news picked up at business and professional conventions, and contacts with present and former employees of companies you count among your prospects.

Prior knowledge about the interviewer's background and personality pays off. It will be so much easier to establish a good rapport with the person who interviews you if you have familiarized yourself with his achievements, special interests, hobbies, likes and dislikes, and even his biases, if any. Generally, the more you know about your interviewer and what makes him tick, the better. The time-honored campus adage, "To earn higher grades, study the teacher, not just the subject" holds good here as well. Since comparatively few job seekers take the trouble to spend time on pre-interview research about the company they are applying to and the interviewer, your efforts in this direction put you miles ahead of the competition.

Rule 2.   Present a Positive Attitude

First and foremost, approach the interview as a winner—not a loser. Preparation plus self-confidence will do it.

If you have had a string of interviews that have gone against you, don't let your attitude be, "Well, here's another one that won't turn out!" This is tantamount to a death wish.

When you step into an interviewer's office weighed down by fear of rejection, you are licked from the very start. I can almost guarantee you that such an attitude will manifest itself negatively in diverse ways—your power of reasoning, your appearance, your posture, how you walk, sit, how you use your voice, even your attempt at a smile.

You start off on the wrong foot if you cast a jaundiced eye on the entire interviewing process, regarding it as an unpleasant if not a demeaning experience—something you are being forced to go through to land a job, like being subjected to an interrogation by a hostile prosecutor masquerading as a friendly psychiatrist. This distorted view can make you instinctively dislike the person interviewing you. Even if you suppress it, it will show and the feeling will be reciprocal. Take the view that the relationship between you and the interviewer is based on mutual interests. There is no reason whatever to feel you have to take a subservient role in this one-to-one relationship. After all, he is as much interested in hiring the right person to fill an existing job vacancy as you are in connecting with a good company.

As part of the screening interview procedure, most large firms require you to fill out an employment application form of one kind or another. Those for low-level and "walk-in" positions are quite simple and limited to a comparatively few routine questions, while those for more important positions are considerably more detailed and broader in scope. Irrespective of the level or nature of the position you apply for, you'll be making a tactical mistake if you look down your nose at this preliminary phase of the interview proceedings. A negative attitude of this kind is bound to show up on the application in sloppy handwriting, cross-outs, and careless spelling, thus seriously undermining your chances to make a favorable impression quite regardless of your other qualifications.

Be modest in your claims, but being modest doesn't mean being humble. Don't hesitate to let your interviewer know about your recent accomplishments and future career plans, and how they mesh with the needs of the company. Don't wait for him to pry this information out of you. Tell him. Have faith in your own merits as a person and as a professional.

Rule 3.   Unfreeze Your Face—Smile!

There is an old Chinese saying that goes something like this: "A man without smiling face must not open shop." How true!

When I need gas for my car, I pass up a service station that is practically around the corner from my home. Although I have been living in the same neighborhood for more than two years, I pass up this station because in all this time whenever I stopped for gas, the attendant always looked at me as if he never saw me before. No recognition of any kind, no greeting, no smile. Nothing but a laconic "Fill 'er up?" I now go out of my way to gas up at another station more than a mile away. Why? Because the quality of gas is any better or the price lower? No. The one and only reason is that there I am always greeted with a friendly smile and jovial hello when I pull up. As they say, a smile changes strangers into friends. It has the same affect on interviewers.

When going for an interview, "think happy." Let a smile grace your face. Smile when you announce yourself to the receptionist and when you meet the interviewer—a deep-down warm smile that comes from the heart and puts a twinkle in your eye. A smile in any language says, "I like you. I'm happy to meet you." What's more, it's guaranteed to improve your looks 100%.

You can almost see a smile on the phone. No wonder that public-minded firms are so choosy about who is assigned to handle the switchboard. "The voice with a smile," to use the old Bell Telephone slogan, is identified with a friendly personality and the type of organization you like to do business with. And that's precisely the image to project when speaking to a would-be employer on the phone or in an actual interview situation. Try it; it works wonders!

Rule 4.   Shake Hands Firmly

A great deal has been written about the technique of shaking hands. Much ado about nothing, you might say; yet, it's surprising how few people really know how or remember to shake hands properly. In ever so many interview evaluation forms, I come across the notation "limp, awkward handshake." The pity of it is that the candidate is often unaware of the poor impression this makes on the interviewer.

A firm, flat-of-palm-against-flat-of-palm handshake, thumbs crossed, with a sensation of gentle pressure, is an outward sign of strength of character—a gesture that invites trust and friendship. A Uriah Heep fingertip handshake is indicative of a person lacking in moral stamina and self-assurance—someone who doesn't quite trust you, or himself. Which image do you want to project in a job interview?

Believe it or not, a handshake—the simple act that it is—requires practice. Political figures have through long experience become adept at "pressing the flesh" as a way of making friends and influencing people. You can do the same.

Rule 5.   Listen Attentively

Hearing is not listening; you hear with your ears, you listen with your mind.

In the world of business, inept listening can bring about confusion and misunderstanding, resulting in catastrophically costly boners. It is for this reason that a growing number of corporations regard the skill of listening as one of the prerequisites for success in business. Sperry Corporation, for example, goes to great expense to provide in-service seminars to upgrade the listening skills of their key personnel in sales management and production.

In a job interview situation, unless you listen attentively, you'll be missing out on one of the most important elements looked for in a candidate. To listen attentively you must show a sustained interest in what the interviewer is saying and not be deflected by what you're going to say next or what you happen to be thinking about at the moment.

This applies not only to interviewing but to other interpersonal relationships as well, as exemplified by the following humorous, but true, vignettes.

Customer to soda fountain clerk: "I'd like a chocolate soda, please."

Clerk: "Sure, what flavor?"

(He heard, but was obviously thinking about something else.)

Here is one in which it was *I* who played the role of the non-listener.

New York City cab drivers, as everybody knows, like to talk a lot, either out of sheer boredom or to take the passenger's eye off the meter. Usually it's the driver who initiates the subject which he hopes will turn into a lively discussion. At this time, for some perverse reason, I wanted to preempt that privilege. It was in the summer during the height of the baseball season, and the games being a timely topic, I off-handedly asked the driver (in the prescribed vernacular), "How're the Yanks doin'?", to which he replied, "Tie score." Without thinking or listening, my next question was, "Favor who?". On hearing this, the driver adjusted his rear view mirror to get a better look at me, scratched his head in slight bewilderment and stepped on the accelerator to get me to my destination as fast as he could. I confess, my mind was not on baseball at the time. In fact, I was not listening to my own questions, nor was I the least bit interested in his reply!

To sharpen your skill in listening, bear in mind the following:

- When the interviewer speaks, look directly at him, eyeball-to-eyeball. Let him see that you're interested in what he's saying. Not only will you establish a better rapport with him but you'll make him feel like he's a great conversationalist.

- For best listening, sit fairly upright in your chair, leaning slightly forward towards the interviewer. Don't slouch in your seat lackadaisically, as if you were watching TV in your easy chair at home. Good posture is a prerequisite to good listening.

- Bridle your thoughts to keep them from racing ahead of what the interviewer is saying. We normally think five times faster than we speak. If he seems momentarily at a loss for the right word to convey a thought or finish a sentence, don't rush to bail him out. This uncalled-for rescue will in no way endear you to him. He could find it embarrassing because it shows that he cannot think as fast, or express himself as well, as you do.

- Don't argue mentally. Though not openly expressed, this state of mind sets up a barrier to good listening.

- React to ideas, not to the person. As a job applicant, you should be ever alert to what the interviewer is saying, not how he acts or what he looks like. Don't let a personal eccentricity (physical or otherwise) distract you to the extent where you no longer listen. A friend of mine, a fellow author, told me that he was once so taken by the odd mannerisms of an editor he was conferring with that he found himself more involved with watching him than paying heed to what he was saying. It seemed that this editor had the most peculiar habit of sticking out his tongue all the way to the side of his mouth every so often, apparently as an aid to better concentration. My friend confessed to me that throughout the conference he couldn't help but keep a lookout for when next that tongue would emerge. As a result, the conference turned out to be not as productive as it might have been because, being intrigued by this odd behavior, he missed the gist of what the editor was trying to convey.

- Rid yourself of visual distractions. To keep your mind focussed on the interviewer's part of the dialogue don't toy with your glasses, pen, or any other object likely to compete with proper listening. While it's alright to take notes during the interview, don't let this deteriorate into idle doodling, thereby tuning out listening. Without being aware of it, you may find yourself abstractedly studying the pattern on the carpet, the scenic view outside the window, or that lipstick smudge on the wall and get to pondering how in the world it got there.

- Listen with animation to show an active interest in what the interviewer is saying. Respond to what you hear by appropriate changes in facial expression. Don't sit there like a klutz. You can nod your head occasionally or verbally indicate your emotional response with such remarks as, "I know exactly what you mean," "I'm glad you mentioned that," or "I don't think I fully realized that before." If you are young at heart and what you're listening to is new and exciting, an exuberant "Wow!" would not be out of order and could be very complimentary.

Rule 6.   Be Mindful of the Physical Appearance You Project

Professional interviewers may not openly admit it (although they do so among themselves) that many job applicants are rejected from further consideration because of poor appearance, regardless of their other qualifications. Surveys show that one out of three applicants are turned down because of either shoddy or inappropriate dress, neglect in grooming, or poor posture.

Hardly ever will an astute interviewer make a direct reference in your presence to any such personal shortcomings for fear of leaving himself open to allegations of discrimination. He is on much safer ground to reject you for technical reasons—being "overqualified," "underqualified," "misqualified"—for the particular job vacancy.

Statistics bear out the fact that applicants who look good are hired faster, get better jobs, and generally start off with higher salaries. If you are not one of those lucky enough to have been endowed by nature with a perfect figure and features, there's still much you can do to enhance your appearance by good grooming and the right selection of clothes.

In Chapter 4 you were given a rather detailed rundown of what constitutes appropriate attire and good grooming. You would do well to go over this once more before your next interview. The total image you project can spell the difference between being bumped in the initial screening interview or given a stamp of approval to go on to the next step—the selection or hiring interview—to meet the person with authority to say, "You're the one we're looking for. When can you start?"

Rule 7.   Show Enthusiasm

If you are vitally concerned about attaining your career goal and are out to land the job that will lead you nearer to that goal, don't put reins on your enthusiasm. Show it and share it with your interviewer.

It's always nice to be in the presence of people who are happily excited about the world around them, life in general, and specifically about their jobs. You can be sure the interviewer will be the first to recognize that quality in you. He may have just gotten through interviewing a string of lackluster candidates who, though qualified in many respects, bored him to death. What a refreshing change it would be for him to meet someone like you who, in addition to possessing the basic qualifications for the job, exudes a spirit of enthusiasm.

Not long ago I mailed out a questionnaire to 2500 personnel managers and employers, in which one of the questions was, "In terms of personal attributes (from a list of 10), what do you look for most in a job candidate?" Of the 1650 who replied, 1175 ranked enthusiasm first.

"Without a spirit of enthusiasm, nothing great has ever been achieved," said Ralph Waldo Emerson. Enthusiasm manifests itself in ever so many ways—your animated speech, eloquent hand and facial gestures, an infectious effervescence when you discuss your ambition and career goal. It's also reflected in your response to what the interviewer says about himself and the firm he represents.

Rule 8.   Approach the Question of Salary Cautiously

Never rush to say okay to the first salary offer, even if it's more than you expected. When the interviewer brings up the question of salary, it indicates that to his way of thinking you are a serious candidate for the job. Start off with the premise that salaries in 8 out of 10 cases are flexible and negotiable. Your leverage depends on the extent you succeed in impressing the interviewer with your above-average qualifications and what they are worth to his company. This holds true for almost all crafts and occupations, even those in traditionally unionized industries where salaries are pegged to a fixed base-pay schedule—printing, construction, interstate trucking, or the automobile industry, for examples. They can pay you more, but they can't pay you less than the contract stipulates. Salary negotiation is the widely accepted practice in the entertainment field—the legitimate theater, motion pictures, radio, and TV. In fact, here as elsewhere, one's professional standing among his peers is measured by how high a salary he can command "above scale."

Salaries in routine low-paying jobs are inclined to be non-negotiable, more often than not on a "take-it-or-leave-it" basis. Not so for high-tech or managerial and executive positions. Here personal negotiations (or, to put it bluntly, haggling) is the name of the game. An experienced interviewer almost always expects it. Don't disappoint him. He probably resorted to the same tactics when he was being interviewed for the position he now holds.

Sooner or later the interviewer will come to that point of the proceedings when the discussion of salary arises. He may put the question to you outright ("What salary are you asking for?"), or be less specific ("What money package do you have in mind?"). However he phrases it, don't tell him. Hedge. Get him to make you an offer first. It's easy to see why you're better off pursuing this course of action. If you're the one to state a figure, it could conceivably be so far out of range as to put you out of the running entirely, or looking at it the other way, so low that you unnecessarily cheat yourself. In the latter instance, the interviewer may have been prepared to offer considerably more, but you don't really expect him to go beyond the figure you ask for, do you?

Should you find yourself in a situation where despite your earlier resolve you are pressed to name a salary forthright, what then? Not to worry. The game is not lost. Strategy still holds sway. You can counter with, "Mr. Employer, as you know, I want this job and believe I am the person you are looking for. I will be better able to name a salary figure after we go over in greater detail the responsibilities the job calls for." This does not seem to be an unreasonable request to make, but entre nous, it is a tactical delay—a stall—to give you time to size up the situation better from all angles and gauge the extent of his interest in you as a prospective employee. If it all seems to stack up in your favor, you're in a good spot. Name a figure that can be negotiated downward if necessary—a concession that will make the interviewer look good in the eyes of his superiors as an effective bargaining agent for the company. Labor negotiators on both sides of the table follow this course of action in order to reach a compromise where both sides show some flexibility and each comes out a winner.

Here are some practical pointers to keep in mind when making a salary decision.

- As part of your pre-interview research, scan the classified ads in newspapers and trade publications to see what salaries other companies are paying for the same or related type of work. Additional sources of information on current salaries in your field are periodically listed in the *National Employment Business Weekly*, a supplement of *The Wall Street Journal*, published by Dow Jones & Company.

- Ask anyone you know who is (or was) an employee of the company or its competitors whether the salary you have in mind is in line with the current salary structure in your field.

- The greater your arsenal of options in the form of other attractive job offers, or the more unique skills you possess which the company needs, the more aggressive you can be in your salary negotiations. In this fortuitous situation, you can be the one to call the shots. Proceed with caution, but set your sites high, with a view of reaching a compromise figure if necessary.

- In all salary matters, follow the universal credo of good salesmanship: ''An experienced salesman doesn't sell, he creates a situation where the customer is eager to buy.'' To get the best salary offer for high-level managerial positions, talk to the interviewer about what interests him most—expanding markets, lower production costs, greater efficiency, improved customer relations, higher profits. These are some of the most beautiful phrases in the corporate language. Show him what you can do to help bring these about. Make him want you!

- For salaries in more routine-type jobs you can put the spotlight on work proficiency and know-how, as well as on such personal traits as integrity, loyalty, punctuality—all impressive attributes that every company looks for in an employee.

- Let your salary history and past performance speak for you. Bear in mind that if you are unemployed (and have been so for a length of time), your ability to negotiate salary is appreciably reduced. Even so, try for a starting salary at least equal to that of what you had last earned on your previous job.

- If you are thinking of switching jobs, then a 20 to 30% increase would be a reasonable goal to strive for. Your best credential is a successful track record. Everybody loves a winner.

- Never, never yield to the temptation to lie about your salary. Not only is it morally wrong, but the interviewer can easily check on your claims. All he has to do is get in touch with your previous employer for verification, or more directly ask to see a copy of your tax returns for the last year or two.

- Before agreeing to any salary offer, realistically calculate your present needs in terms of fixed expenses to maintain your accustomed lifestyle. Don't fail to give some thought to a rising cost of living, or such anticipated expenses in the foreseeable future as tuition for your teenagers about to enter college, plans for home improvement, rising mortgage payments, and so forth.

- If you can't come to an amicable agreement on salary, don't turn the job down summarily. Ask for a reasonable time to reconsider the offer.

- Most companies have an established salary range for each category of work. Negotiate for the upper range.

- If you possess unique skills the company is looking for, the interviewer will go out of his way to meet your salary demands even if only to lure you away from competitors in the field.

- You have greater latitude in salary negotiations if the job you're being interviewed for represents a position especially created for you since a fixed salary may not as yet have been determined. There are no precedents to stand in your way.

Rule 9.   Don't Talk Too Much and Talk Yourself Out of a Job

Prominently displayed on the wall of a sport fishermen's clubhouse there is a prized taxidermist-stuffed barracuda. Below it is the following inscription: "I would not be up here now if I hadn't opened my mouth so often."

Remember that fish next time you find yourself talking too much in a job interview.

Professional interviewers are by training disposed to apportion 75% of interview time to the applicant and 25% to themselves. The theory behind this prescribed ratio is to give the applicant free reign to talk about himself, and in so doing reveal certain facets of his background, both professional and personal, not shown in his resume or which may not normally surface through questioning. As an applicant, it is to your advantage to reverse this ratio or at least to balance it so that you can learn as much as possible about the particular job you are applying for, the company, and, tangentially, about the interviewer himself.

You can learn more by listening than talking. This does not mean that you should take a passive role in the interview proceedings. By all means, speak up and show how your qualifications mesh in with the requirements of the job. Boast a little—there is no one to do it for you—but don't hog the show.

Resolve never to talk about yourself more than 60 seconds at a time. Adroitly ask the interviewer questions relative to specific points in the discussion. If at times a gap in the dialogue develops when neither you nor he is holding forth, don't panic even though the few moments of silence (like those caused by temporary technical difficulties on TV) seem like an eternity. Learn how to handle silence, turning it into a looked-for opportunity to collect your thoughts and mentally edit what you are going to say next when the line opens up. A pause now and then is not only refreshing to the ear, but helps to add emphasis to a point in a conversation.

When you and the interviewer have come to a tentative understanding of points agreed upon in the discussion, shut up. Don't keep on talking, keep on talking, keep on talking. Know when the party is over. At this time don't add anything that has already been said and concluded which could conceivably bring up new issues or reveal unresolved doubts in the mind of the interviewer. After-thought utterances such as, "By the way . . . ," "Incidentally . . . ," "I meant to ask you . . . ," or "This reminds me . . ." unnecessarily prolong the interview and can negate the good impression you've made so far. The danger in this is that the job within your grasp—the one that's just right for you—can slip through your fingers.

Don't let this happen to you.

Rule 10.   Never Create a Situation Where You Keep the Interviewer Waiting

There are many good and valid reasons for arriving late to an interview, but the best of them won't help you when you show up a half-hour or even fifteen minutes beyond the scheduled time.

Arriving late to a job interview, for whatever reason, forces you to start off with an apology. That's bad. If you go to an extended alibi, that's worse. Should you fail to show up at all and not even bother to telephone, that's absolutely unconscionable. Could you fault the interviewer for reasoning that if you fail to show up on time to the interview, you can't be expected to show up on time on the job?

To make sure you won't be late for the interview, anticipate the unanticipated. Take into consideration possible situations that may arise to delay you along the way, and allow an extra margin of time just in case.

SITUATION: Your interview was scheduled for 10 in the morning and the 8:35 commuter express you had figured on taking to get you in on time was delayed by 18 minutes. You did not consider that as a possibility, did you?

SITUATION: You could have sworn that the address was 385 *East* 57th Street. You arrived right on time only to discover (to your utter dismay) that the address really is 385 *West* 57th Street, and at this hour it takes an interminable time to get across town.

SITUATION: Your car, a go-getter in any weather, this winter morning refuses to budge or even purr because of a run-down battery, and requires a boost to come to life again. You're stuck waiting over an hour for the AAA service truck to come to your rescue.

SITUATION: On the way to the interview, you are lost and find yourself in unfamiliar territory with all traffic signs going one way—the opposite direction you are heading for. This involves numerous time-consuming detours to get to your destination.

SITUATION: You scheduled a 9 A.M. interview and another one at 10:15. The first interview runs well past the time you expected it to take and you had dovetailed the two of them practically back-to-back. Unfortunately both interviews are geographically miles apart, causing you to show up 40 minutes late for the second interview.

SITUATION: Your alarm clock didn't go off and you overslept, and you got up late and . . .

But why go on?

Whatever the reason for showing up late, one thing is sure: The interview will go down-hill from the very start, no matter how qualified you are technically, academically, or otherwise.

Supposing when you get to the interview you are told that the interviewer is 15 to 20 minutes behind schedule. Don't regard this delay with visible (or suppressed) annoyance. Rather look upon it as a fortuitous happenstance to give you a chance to once more review your resume and other credentials as well as the list of questions you prepared to ask the interviewer. You could also browse through the company's Annual Report, newsletter or other trade publication usually found on reception room coffee-tables. You would indeed be guilty of misuse of time just sitting there doing nothing at all or finishing the morning's crossword puzzle or absorbing yourself in the sports section of your newspaper.

Indirectly, from an entirely different point of view, it could turn out to be in your favor if asked to wait. In greeting you, the person interviewing you may be psychologically impelled to find ways to make up to you for having kept you on hold. Any way you look at it, you're infinitely better off if the circumstances are such that the interviewer has kept *you* waiting rather than the other way around.

Rule 11. Get the Interviewer to Like You

Many an interviewer, after carefully weighing the pros and cons of a candidate's total qualifications, ends up basing his hiring decision not on a purely objective appraisal but on a gut feeling he has about him. When all is said and done, the interviewer is not infrequently guided by a little inner voice that prompts him to say, "I just feel this guy (or gal) is right for the job."

How can a candidate—specifically *you*—get the interviewer to feel that way about you?

First and foremost, be mindful of what you say and how you act to foster his sense of importance without appearing to patronize him. All of us have an inner need for appreciation and praise—you, I, and the more than four billion other souls in the world. Here is what William James, the eminent American philosopher, had to say about this universal need: "The deepest principle in human nature is the craving to be appreciated." Mind you, he called this a *craving*, not merely a "need." John Dewey, the dean of educational philosophy, echoed the same sentiment, but put it another way: "The desire to feel important," he said, "is the deepest urge in human nature."

As an illustration of this, the story is told about the once imperious Kaiser Wilhelm II, who after the devastating defeat of Germany in World War I became a man without a country and the most despised individual throughout the world. He sought refuge in Holland to save his life. To say the least, his self-esteem was completely shattered. The former Kaiser was the personification of evil to everyone—everyone, that is, except to one little boy who sent him a glowing letter assuring him of his undiminished admiration, regardless of what the world thought about him. The Kaiser, deeply touched to learn that someone, somewhere, still held such an exalted opinion of him, invited the youngster to visit him—which he did, accompanied by his mother, whom the Kaiser subsequently married.

Sam Himmell, Chairman of the Baldwin Paper Company, in his book, *Baldwin Brevities*, tells an amusing anecdote worth repeating. Two newlyweds were honeymooning in Atlantic City. As they walked arm-in-arm along the beach, the young groom turned to the ocean and lyrically cried out, "Roll on! Thou deep and dark blue ocean—roll on!" His starry-eyed bride gazed at the water for a moment, then looking at him admiringly, in hushed tones gasped, "Oh, Sheldon, you wonderful man! It's doing it!!" (She instinctively sensed how to make him feel important.)

If you've made an effort to research your interviewer prior to meeting with him, you are in a better strategic position to direct the conversation to things he would like to hear—anything to add support to his self-esteem. You might allude to some complimentary news item about him or the company he represents that you came across in a recent issue of a trade publication or the business section of the newspaper. Perhaps you recall reading about the active part he played in a professional seminar or other business function of the kind. With no pre-researched material to go by, you may make reference to the sensitive position he holds with the company and how much his acumen and expertise must count in the recruitment of the right personnel. Or else you may want to make mention of the courtesy shown to you by the friendly secretary or receptionist you chatted with briefly prior to the interview. You may find something nice to say about the impressive citations displayed on the wall, or the aesthetic décor of the office or reception room. A word of caution: In all this, avoid obvious flattery. Unless you sincerely believe what you say and express it without gushing, don't say it. You'll identify yourself as an artful sycophant. Flattery comes from the lips; praise, from the heart.

Never, never upstage the interviewer in any manner whatsoever. Nobody expects you to be humble (indeed it would be detrimental to your cause if you acted that way), but by the same token don't act the know-it-all and inflate your ego to the extent where he's pushed to the dark side of the moon. Make him feel important and be ready to defer to his better judgment when the occasion calls for it.

If you want the interviewer to like you, show that you are interested in what he's saying by listening responsively. In the cross-current of topics that come up in the interview, resist the temptation to interrupt him or, worse still, prove him to be wrong. If you do, you may have your moment of glory but it will be short-lived, and is bound to work against you no matter how right you are and how wrong he is.

Bear in mind, a person's name is to him the sweetest sound there is. You start off right when you address the interviewer by name (and tell him yours) when introduced to him and refer to him by it from time to time during the course of the interview. Be sure to check with the receptionist before meeting the interviewer about the proper pronunciation of his name. Hold off calling him by his first name until he suggests that you do so, as the relationship between you two warms up.

Andrew Carnegie, the steel magnate of this century, early in life recognized that people are made to feel important by being remembered by name. He is quoted as saying that he attributed a good part of his success in business to remembering the names of his legion of business associates, and the thousands of workers in his mills as well. Franklin D. Roosevelt knew that one of the best ways to gain good will and make people feel important was to remember the names of the multitudes of people he came in contact with during the course of his long political career.

Show the interviewer the courtesy and respect due him by virtue of the position he holds with the company and the role he plays in the hiring process—as it affects your career. Simply put, if you want him to like you, you must like him—and show him that you do.

Ideally, an interview is a symbiosis—an affable relationship between two parties; in this case, you, the job applicant, and the person interviewing you.

Summing it all up: It is a known fact that the candidate who comes out of the interview with a job offer is not necessarily the one best qualified technically, important an attribute as that may be, but the one who makes the best impression.

Here is a recap of the 11 cardinal rules for successful job interviews, which if applied with discretion will, all things being equal, turn the tide in your favor.

Show That You Are Knowledgeable About the Company and Its Operation

Interviewers are inclined to look with favor on a job applicant who has made an effort to research the company he wishes to connect with. As the applicant, it will help you get a better grasp of the company structure and at the same time you will be better prepared to let your interviewer know in what ways you can contribute to the company's growth.

Present a Positive Attitude

Self-doubts and fear of failure can scuttle a job interview. Put yourself in the employer's place. Would you hire someone exhibiting such traits? If you come to an interview like a nebbish, you'll be treated like one.

Unfreeze Your Face. Smile!

A smile improves your looks 100% and helps to engender a cordial relationship between you and the interviewer. See what a difference a smile and a friendly disposition that goes with it can make next time you find yourself in an interview situation.

Shake Hands Firmly

Whether you realize it or not, the interviewer is likely to be influenced by the manner in which a job applicant shakes hands. A firm handshake suggests a sense of purpose and strength of character.

Listen Attentively

To show that you are listening attentively and as a mark of respect, look at the interviewer directly when he speaks. Avoid visual and mental distractions.

Be Mindful of the Physical Appearance You Project

To be regarded as a success, it pays to make a special effort to fit the successful image—in what you wear and in your grooming. Attractive men and women invariably get preferential treatment when it comes to the hiring process and salary offers.

Show Enthusiasm

Nothing is ever accomplished without a spirit of enthusiasm. Enthusiasm adds luster to any personality and is a vital ingredient to success in job procurement, as it is in any line of endeavor.

Approach the Question of Salary Cautiously

Never say okay to the first salary offer, even if it's more than you expected. If you can't get all you ask for, see how far you can go through channels of negotiation.

Don't Talk Too Much and Talk Yourself Out of a Job

Sense when the interview is over. Don't linger. Close while you're ahead, but don't neglect to ask for the job.

Never Create a Situation Where You Keep the Interviewer Waiting

Showing up late to an interview, thereby upsetting the interviewer's appointment schedule, is unforgivable. Sure as anything, the interview will go downhill from the very start, regardless of your alibi.

Get the Interviewer to Like You

You can do so by making him feel important by what you say and how you act. Adopting this strategy, he'll be beholden to you and not even realize why.

Darling
Good News !!!   4:30

Lillian Henderson, exec V.P. of Stanley-Furman Associates (the firm you interviewed several weeks ago) phoned, to let you know that you have been selected as the #1 choice as Director of Marketing Research.
She left word for you to call her office tomorrow morning—

Rita

The culmination of a successful interview—and a little note that makes it all worthwhile . . .

14

INTERVIEW FOLLOW-UP

THE PERSON WHO interviews you deserves to be thanked for the time he has set aside to meet with you. In addition to a verbal expression of appreciation at the end of the interview, it's good practice to follow up with a brief thank-you note or phone call, even if you've been turned down or put on hold. Don't procrastinate. Do it within a few days before the interviewer's impression of you begins to fade or blend in with the other candidates he may have seen.

Do you want to be in a class by yourself? Consider sending a Western Union Mailgram® as a followup to an interview. It can serve as an effective attention-getter and is distinguishingly different from ordinary mail to get special notice. In a sense, a Mailgram® is a letter made to look like and have the visual impact of a telegram. You can dictate your message via the telephone. It is guaranteed to be delivered by the Postal Service to reach the interviewer's desk the following morning.

Do you know that most applicants, especially those who don't succeed in getting a job offer right off the bat, don't bother to thank the interviewer once they've left the office? Not that they are inherently discourteous or are lacking in good manners. It simply doesn't occur to them that this is the proper thing to do.

Be different! Single yourself out in this respect and in so doing you'll put yourself in a more favorable light than your competition. All things considered, the social amenities you demonstrate in a followup of your interview can turn the tide in your favor and make you the #1 contender for the job.

There is more than a matter of social amenities involved here, as important as that is. A post interview followup has its practical aspects as well:

- It permits you to reinforce the good impression you made on the interviewer.

- It's a good way to clear up any misunderstanding that might have come up during the course of the interview.

- It serves as a means of reaffirming your unique qualifications for the job.

- A post-interview thank-you letter gives you an opportunity to include additional data (news clippings, photocopies of samples of your work, printouts of sales records) alluded to in the interview but which you may not have had on hand at the time.

- It serves as a reminder that you want the job and are eager to become affiliated with the company.

KEEPING TRACK OF INTERVIEWS

In an extended job-search campaign it is assumed that you will go through dozens of interviews before the job that's right for you materializes. To keep track of all these interviews, it is necessary to devise a practical system for recording pertinent data for both followups and future prospecting. This shouldn't prove difficult. All you need to set up a recordkeeping system of this kind is a pack or two of index cards and file box to go with it, plus the temperament of a reporter-bookkeeper. These cards can be typed or pre-printed to include such headings as: position applied for, name and address of company, name and title of interviewer, name of secretary or receptionist, date and time of interview, and outcome of interview. Add other headings that you feel are important. A filing system such as suggested here is shown on page 99.

During the course of the interview (or right after you leave the office), jot down in your little notebook matters relating to salary, benefits that go with it, answers to questions you prepared to ask the interviewer, when or if additional interviews are forthcoming, and so forth. Don't wait until you get home. By that time you may have gone through several other interviews with different companies. Facts have a way of becoming scrambled at the end of a full, drag-out day. Don't rely on memory. Write it down. As Confucius says, "Short pencil better than long memory."

Upon returning home, assiduously transcribe your hastily written notes onto your followup index cards—one card for each interview. On the reverse side you may wish to jot down your personal impressions of the interviewer, the company, and anything else which will help to fix in your mind the highlights of the interview. You can freely do so much the same way as you would in a personal diary. There's no one to stop you from giving a brief word-picture of some unique characteristic to better identify the interviewer—perhaps something about his appearance, mannerism of speech or behavior, his tendency to stoop to compensate for his 6′3″

,height, the affected Oxford accent he put on to impress you—and in a more serious vein, the visceral feeling you have about the job.

Somewhere on the card, it's helpful to symbolically indicate your total assessment of the job prospect, using a star-rating system such as critics sometimes resort to when graphically evaluating a motion picture:

    ****   (Hot prospect, excellent potential.)
    ***   (Looks good, follow up.)
    **   (Only fair, keep in touch.)
    *   (Slim chance, but you can never tell.)

Bear this in mind: Any system you devise (and conscientiously adhere to) to keep track of your past and future contacts in your job-search is infinitely better than relying on the vagaries of memory.

RECORD OF INTERVIEW

NAME OF COMPANY : _Metro Display and Exhibit Corporation_

ADDRESS : _738 West 37th St. N.Y.C._   PHONE : _971-9361_

TYPE OF BUSINESS OR SERVICE : _Display designers for the pharmaceutical trade_

INTERVIEWER'S NAME : _Stanley Rice, Jr._   TITLE : _V.P. in charge of production_

NAME OF SECRETARY OR ASSISTANT : _Miss Jean Hess (Rice's executive secretary)_

DATE OF INTERVIEW : _Thurs. 2/9/82_ TIME : _9:15 A.M._ WHERE HELD : _Room 409_

POSITION APPLIED FOR : _Creative Director, Window Display Dept._

RESULT OF INTERVIEW : _Mr. Rice was impressed with my resume and portfolio, but said he is presently considering two other applicants and will come to a decision within two weeks. He asked me to contact him at that time._

PERSONAL IMPRESSION OF THE INTERVIEWER : _Mr. Rice was courteous and soft spoken. The son of the founder of the firm, he is a graduate of Pratt, my own alma mater._

FOLLOW UP : _Within a day or two, send him a thank you note. Phone him Monday, 2/23 A.M._

RECORD OF INTERVIEW

NAME OF COMPANY

ADDRESS   PHONE

TYPE OF BUSINESS

DATE AND TIME OF INTERVIEW

NAME OF PERSON WHO INTERVIEWED ME   TITLE

SECRETARY'S NAME   HIRING DECISION MADE BY

POSITION APPLIED FOR   DEPARTMENT

INTERVIEW AS RESULT OF

OUTCOME OF INTERVIEW

FOLLOW-UP

PERSONAL IMPRESSION OF THE INTERVIEWER

(OVER)

REFERRALS

NAME OF PERSON TO CONTACT:_____

ADDRESS: _____   PHONE:_____

REFERRED BY:_____   DATE: _____

REFERRAL'S RELATIONSHIP TO ME :_____

NATURE OF REQUEST:_____

_____

REPLY : _____

_____

_____

FOLLOW-UP DATA: _____

_____

_____

_____

April 10, 1987

Mr. Ron Sperber, President
Sperber & Company
132 Park Avenue South
New York, New York 10003

Dear Ron:

This is to let you know how much I appreciate the opportunity
you have given me to meet with you regarding the position as
District Sales Manager of the Window Display Division of
Sperber & Company. I have long been aware of the fine reputation of your organization and would be proud indeed to be
associated with it.

You may recall, Ron, in our discussion of several days ago,
my mentioning an article I wrote scheduled to appear in the
forthcoming issue of Visual Merchandising. In it I singled
out Sperber & Co., as one of the outstanding innovators in
the industry. In the thought you'd like to use the article
for promotional purposes, I am forwarding you by special de-
livery an advance copy of the magazine.

I'll contact you early next week to see how close you've come
to a hiring decision.

Sincerely,

John Stanford

John Stanford

EXAMPLE OF FOLLOW-UP LETTER

Dorothy Williams
420-05 Central Road
Cincinnati, Ohio 45420

February 20, 1987

Mr. Charles D. Seabury, Vice Pres.
American Savings & Loan Assoc.
428 Gilbert Avenue
Cincinnati, Ohio 45202

Dear Mr. Seabury:

It was kind of you to arrange my introduction to Mr. Rand,
Senior Systems Analyst of Computer Graphics. I met with
him yesterday, and from the way the interview went, it looks
promising that I'll get the job.

Mr. Seabury, please know that whether the job materializes
or not, I owe you a sincere vote of thanks for your interest
in me.

Will keep you posted,

Yours truly,

Dorothy Williams

Dorothy Williams

EXAMPLE OF FOLLOW-UP LETTER OF THANKS FOR REFERRAL

```
┌─────────────────────────────┬──────────────────────────────────┐
│  MILDRED SANFORD             │  ⊔⊔⊔  ⊔⊔⊔   ⊔⊔⊔   ⊔⊔⊔           │
│  142 N. MAPLE AVENUE         │                                  │
│  GREENWICH, CT 06830         │  western union  western union  western union │
└─────────────────────────────┴──────────────────────────────────┘
```

1-020059C231 04/15/84 TLX WU MKTG GWH MIAA
 01 GREENWICH CT 081982

GERALD M. PORTER, PRES.
KING ASSOCIATES INC.
147 STANDISH RD
STAMFORD CT 06902

APRIL 15, 1987

MR. GERALD M. PORTER, PRES.
KING ASSOCIATES, INC.
147 STANDISH RD
STAMFORD, CT 06902

DEAR MR. PORTER,

THANKS EVER SO MUCH FOR THE TIME YOU HAVE TAKEN TO INTERVIEW
ME AS YOUR PROSPECTIVE COMPANY CONTROLLER.

HAVING HAD THE OPPORTUNITY TO DISCUSS THIS POSITION WITH YOU
IN GREATER DEPTH, I AM ALL THE MORE EAGER TO BECOME AFFILIATED
WITH YOUR FINE ORGANIZATION AND AM CONFIDENT THAT I AM THE
PERSON YOU'RE LOOKING FOR.

SHOULD I NOT HEAR FROM YOU WITHIN A WEEK OR SO, I WILL TAKE
THE LIBERTY OF CONTACTING YOU TO SEE HOW THINGS STAND.

SINCERELY,

MILDRED SANFORD
142 N MAPLE AVENUE
GREENWICH, CT 06830

13:50 EST

MGMCOMP

EXAMPLE OF MAILGRAM® – TYPE FOLLOW-UP LETTER

15

SHOPPING LIST OF BENEFITS AND PERKS

Your base salary—that is, the check you take home at the end of the week—provides for routine day-to-day expenditures: food, clothing, car, rent or mortgage payments, utilities, tuition for the kids, entertainment, and all other things that collectively set your lifestyle. Fringe benefits and perks (short for perquisites), such as insurance plans, bonuses, vacations, employee discounts, stock options, and profit-sharing plans, can amount to as much as 40% above base salary. This represents the frosting on the cake. As a full-time company employee, you are either automatically entitled to some of these as standard company-bestowed benefits that go with the job, or else you have to negotiate for them. How far you can get will depend largely upon flexibility of corporate policy and the extent of your bargaining power.

The pick of the perks invariably goes to higher-ups on the management and executive level and is the prerogative of those possessing high-demand skills, as well as for those who are privy to important trade formulas, or hold job-related patents. If you were some mythical alchemist who could magically transform lead into gold, you could write your own ticket. Normally, however, all you are entitled to are standard company benefits that are on the books. The rest you have to bargain for. It's up to you to realistically assess your true worth to the company to know how far you can go. If you can't get all you ask for, settle for those that are most important to you.

Here is a rundown of typical fringe benefits and perks to keep in mind when discussing the money-package with your interviewer:

Insurance

Life Insurance: Most companies provide some form of life insurance coverage, either fully financed by the company or on a contributory basis.

Health Insurance: Nearly all well-established firms now offer major medical insurance for employees who've been with the company a prescribed number of years. It is customary for this privilege to be extended (in full or part) to the employee's spouse and in some cases to his underage dependents as well. As time goes on, an increasing number of companies continue to subsidize health insurance for their retired employees.

Dental Insurance: Of late, dental insurance has become an added employee benefit, subsidized to varying degrees by the company.

Sick Leave

Eight to ten days paid sick leave are fairly common, with unused sick leave days banked towards the employee's retirement, or in some other way compensated for.

Vacations

The current general practice is a two-week vacation period after one year of service for rank-and-file employees, and anywhere between three to six weeks for those in middle and upper management rank as well as for employees who have been with the company for a long stretch of 25 years and beyond.

An employee in a key position may be given the privilege to arrange his vacation to coincide with a trade convention or other business conclave scheduled in a city he is especially interested in visiting. Transportation and all costs covering hotel, food, entertainment, admission to center of activities, etc., are chalked up as legitimate business expenses and as such are completely or in part financed by the company. It's not unusual for the company to pick up the tab for the spouse as well if his (or her) presence and participation is deemed to be a business asset.

Pension Plans

The majority of firms offer a choice of pension plans which an employee can select if he has been with the company for 10 years or more. Pensions are generally computed on the highest average salary the employee earns in the last three to five years of service. The vested pension right is not collectable until the employee has reached a stipulated retirement age set by the company.

Cost of Living Adjustment (COLA)

This is a company policy whereby employees' salaries are periodically reviewed and adjusted to reflect the prevailing cost-of-living index—a benefit long enjoyed by most government employees.

Bonuses

Companies traditionally make it a practice to distribute across-the-board bonuses to employees as a token of good will. The amount may vary from an annual Christmas gift of several hundred dollars to many thousands of dollars offered as a cash "front-end" bonus to superachievers in the field as an inducement to join the company.

In addition, top-ranking executives with corporations enjoying a record of jumbo profits are potential recipients of bonuses based on superior performance. These bonuses may range from 20% to 40% of the executives' base salary, payable at the end of each fiscal year.

Stock Options

This is a perk made available to qualified employees who wish to own stock in the company they work for. The company makes this possible by granting loans at interest rates considerably lower than prevailing commercial rates or deferred payment arrangements.

Employee Discounts

It is an established policy followed by nearly all large firms to allow employees a 10% to 25% discount on purchases of company products.

Company-paid Tuition Allowance

Large companies for the most part stand ready to underwrite partial or full tuition costs for any qualified employee planning to continue his education or upgrade his work skills. In some instances, the company does not dictate the course of study, leaving that entirely to the discretion of the employee.

Scholarships for employees' children of school age who qualify academically are in the realm of an additional perk.

Profit Sharing

Today many large corporations make it a practice to offer attractive profit-sharing programs to their high-ranking personnel on the condition that they remain with the company for a stipulated number of years. As time goes on, more and more corporations provide some type of profit-sharing program to all of their employees, regardless of rank. In some instances as much as 10 percent of the corporation's pretax profits are earmarked for this purpose.

Tax-free Gifts

Non-cash gifts (TV's, microwave ovens, home computers, etc.) are offered by some companies to employees in acknowledgement of outstanding service. Gifts of this nature are tax-free (currently limited to $400 in market value) and are for IRS records not considered an addition to the employee's basic income.

Relocation Expenses

A key employee scheduled to be transferred to another branch of the company (out of state or in a foreign country) is reimbursed for the varied expenses entailed in moving. In addition, assistance is provided in selling his present home and arranging a mortgage for an equivalent home in the new location. Relocation expenses may also include a cost-of-living differential allowance and, if the job is located in a foreign country, education allowance for children of school age.

Severance Pay

Facetiously referred to as "lump-sum alimony," this is an arrangement in contract form between company and employee, which guarantees the employee a stipulated sum of money if his services are terminated before the expiration of the contract. Such an arrangement is intended to protect both parties. It assures the employer that a high-caliber worker will stay on the job for a specified number of years, and the employee is assured that he will not be arbitrarily dismissed without due compensation.

Capital Accumulation Plan

This represents an additional perk made available to employees to encourage thrift in the form of regular savings. In accordance with this plan the company agrees to match 50% of the employee's contribution (not exceeding 6% of his annual salary). The accumulated sum is held for him in escrow, redeemable upon completion of a specified number of years of service.

Miscellaneous Perks and Benefits

Here is a sampling of the crème de là crème perks and special benefits reserved for key personnel in the higher salary bracket.

- A brand new prestige automobile every year for business and personal use.

- Company-paid club membership privileges covering dues, club fees, and unlimited use of facilities.

- Yearly medical check-up for executives over forty.

- Reserved executive parking.

- Extended vacations with full pay.

- Generous front-end bonuses.

- Use of company CPA for consultation on personal financial matters as well as free legal counseling by staff attorneys.

- Generous expense accounts.

- Contracts, if requested.

- Opportunity for partnership status.

Summing it up: You, as a company employee, are entitled to the usual state-of-the-art benefits and perks by virtue of corporate policy. Others you have to press for. The greater your accomplishments—the more you've got going for you—the greater your leverage.

16

QUESTION AND ANSWER ROUNDUP

ABOUT PERSONAL APPEARANCE

To give you an idea of what I look like: I am 23, and 5'6'', weighing 235 pounds. With my goatee and expansive girth, I could be taken for a young Burl Ives. My problem is that though I consider myself a highly qualified illustrator, I have been unable to get a job with an advertising agency. In an interview my physical appearance goes against me. I can shave my beard but don't tell me to lose weight—I've tried and failed.

It is a known fact that some employers show a reluctance to put obese job applicants on the payroll as staff members because of possible health risks.

If you've done all you can to reduce with no apparent success, there comes a time when you must accept yourself as you are. Fortified with a positive attitude, and with persistence, I am certain that sooner or later you will encounter a prospective employer who will judge you solely by your skill as an artist. In the meantime, you may want to take on freelance assignments and work from home on a pay-as-you-deliver basis. There is always the possibility that several of your accounts—who get to know you well and are pleased with the quality of your work and service—may offer you a staff job. For that matter, you may eventually decide to open your own agency and become your own boss.

When I applied for a position recently in a prestigious brokerage house, I was aware I got the cold shoulder even before I had an opportunity to discuss my credentials. What might have been the reason?

There could have been several. The one that comes to mind first is your general appearance. Next time before you venture forth to an interview, look at yourself in a full-length mirror. Do you like what you see? While there's very little you can do to radically change your physical appearance on short notice, it is possible to almost overnight effect a marked difference in the total image you present through careful grooming, proper selection of clothes, and good posture.

I've heard that cosmetic surgery on the nose (colloquially referred to as a ''nose job'') could greatly improve one's appearance and self-image. Does this type of surgery leave visible scars?

In the hands of a competent cosmetic surgeon any residual scars are so artfully concealed within the nose as to be practically invisible and do not generally create a problem.

I am 5'5'', and for a man that is somewhat below average height. Is it true that the height of a person has a bearing on his chances for success in the business world? And if so, what can I do about it?

There is no question that taller men project a more authoritative image than those of shorter stature. It's known that they command higher salaries and are promoted faster.

There is not much you can do to increase your actual height once you've reached adulthood, but good posture will help some. Also wearing higher heels (so-called ''elevator shoes'') will make you appear 1½'' to 2'' taller than you really are. If you aren't as tall as you'd like to be, think tall.

Could the beard I've grown lately go against me in a job interview?

It could, unless you are a rock musician, Freudian psychologist, or orthodox rabbi. If it's a routine 9-to-5 position you are applying for—as for example, Assistant Manager of a bank—you'd do better to shave it off, at least for the interview. Once on the job, unless wearing a beard is contrary to corporate policy, you can grow it back if you so wish. All is not lost. If it grew before, it will sprout again.

I've had this problem of poorly aligned teeth as long as I can remember and now feel it's too late for me to start wearing braces like an adolescent. Is there any way of correcting this condition without braces?

A newly developed type of brace that is placed on the *back* of the teeth rather than the front has shown itself effective. It might in your case, too.

DRESS AND
GROOMING

As a recent graduate applying for an Assistant Editor's position, would it be impressive to bring to the interview the gold medal I won in a national competition in creative writing?

No. Just tell the interviewer about it with due modesty. Note of awards of this kind should be of course included in your resume. Medals are excess baggage in an interview.

What do you think about my wearing a Phi Beta Kappa key when interviewing?

It's not recommended, unless perchance you know that the interviewer is likewise a fellow member of Phi Beta Kappa, or the position you're applying for calls for a high academic standing. Under ordinary circumstances it might be looked upon as a showoff gesture.

What's wrong with using a scented cologne as an after-shave lotion when going to an interview?

It's okay if you allow some time to go by before appearing for the interview. By that time the pungent fragrance will have dissipated itself and you won't come in smelling like a rose.

My close friend has a bad case of body odor, a condition she is evidently unaware of when appearing for an interview, but the person interviewing her doesn't have to be told. The pity of it is that without knowing why, she is turned down for many jobs she qualifies for. Should someone tell her? Should I tell her?

You could not consider yourself a true friend if you didn't. You'll be closer to her than ever before if you tell her.

My problem is that although I am past 25, I look like a teenager and don't give the impression of a responsible adult. Consequently, I lose out on a number of good job opportunities.

To avoid a teenage look, select your wardrobe to give you a more mature and sophisticated appearance—a well-fitted business suit rather than a frilly dress and medium or high heel shoes, especially if you're short in stature. Proper hair styling will help too, as well as good posture and a firm step.

When you're 40 or over, you'll wish you looked younger than your age!

How far do you go in makeup when appearing for a job interview?

Moderation is the key word. Go lightly on the intensity of the color lipstick you use. Mascara, discreetly applied, will do much to make your eyes look larger and brighter. Avoid painting your eyes with four or five different shadows like a star performer in the circus or theater. This applies equally well whether you are a candidate for a word-processor's job or for a high executive position in marketing research.

In assessing a woman's wardrobe, is there any difference between style and fashion?

Yes. Style is less faddish than fashion. Fashion tends to change from year to year, whereas style reflects personal taste and is more permanent and "goes" with the stamp of personality of the wearer. Identify yourself with your own style more than with the whims of fashion.

I don't have much hair to speak of. What is left is just a frowzy fringe on the sides–in plain words, I'm a baldhead. Should I resort to a toupee?

If a toupee unmistakably looks like a toupee, don't. An ill-fitted and poorly matched hairpiece only calls attention to itself. It shows up as an ill-concealed deception and defeats its own purpose.

I once overheard a personnel director remark, "I never trust a guy with a toupee." (He was bald himself and did not believe in a cover-up.) Let's put it this way: If a well-fitted, color-matched hairpiece makes you feel younger and improves your looks, wear it.

I am a 25-year-old male in a line of work where youthful good looks is a prerequisite to employment, and being partially bald, I am considering a hair transplant. The several toupees I've tried are now permanently resting on the styrene head-shaped figures on my dresser. I can't get used to toupees because they feel warm and uncomfortable, especially during the summer months. Could a hair transplant solve my problem?

Facetiously, off the top of my head I'm not sure that it will. From what

I've heard, not all hair transplants work out right. It's not as simple as putting sod on a lawn. Hair transplants involve long, drawn-out procedures. Consult a dermatologist or cosmetic surgeon whom you can trust. Better still, talk to anyone you know who has gone through this procedure and see what he has to say. You may conclude after all that bald is beautiful.

Isn't it somewhat misleading to be told time and time again that conservative dress is a must for all applicants, irrespective of the type of job they apply for?

It would appear that way. An applicant for an auto mechanic's job coming to an interview impeccably dressed in the conservative attire generally associated with an IBM executive or a financial consultant would be regarded as an oddity, as would a funeral director in tennis shoes. Every profession and occupation has its own unspoken code of dress. The important thing to remember is, no matter what your particular line of work may be (and the dress considered appropriate for it), you are bound to make a more favorable impression on any interviewer if you are dressed neatly and are well-groomed.

Is a hat part of the prescribed ensemble for the well-dressed male going to a job interview?

No. While in "merrie old England" it may still be customary for a man's business attire to include the traditional derby, in our own country hats for men have long passed out of vogue. Whether hats will ever come back in style is a matter of conjecture, and it is the fervent hope of the men's hat industry of America that that day is not far off.

I've always been partial to bow-ties. For interviewing should I change to a traditional tie, just to conform?

Yes, according to Robert O. Snelling, Chairman of the Board of Snelling & Snelling, one of the world's largest employment agencies. A longtime bow-tie buff himself, he advises his clients to wear a standard tie when dressing for a job interview. Save your favorite bow-tie for formal and other non-business occasions.

When invited to return for a second and third interview, would it be advisable to show up in an entirely different outfit each time?

Not necessarily, but it is better to show some variation in dress, if only a change of accessories.

What do you think the interviewer's reaction would be to a male applicant wearing a decorative wrist bracelet?

That's hard to say. He may come across an interviewer now and then who could possibly regard this type of ornamentation in a man as odd or excessive.

My favorite dress is one which by present standards of fashion is too long and full. How can I affect a change without extensive alterations?

A colorful belt will help anchor the dress to your body, in effect shortening it and at the same time adding a point of contrast color-keyed to your ensemble.

What makes for a successful business wardrobe?

It's been said that the best-dressed people wear forgettable clothes that are smart looking, properly fitted, and never gaudy.

SELF-
EVALUATION

I've read that before starting on an extensive job-search campaign, you should do a study on yourself from the time "way back when" till now, even if it takes 200 to 300 pages of writing, to get to know who you really are and what you want out of life. How do you feel about it?

This procedure has been suggested by Richard N. Bolles in his classic book *What Color Is Your Parachute?*, and confirmed by other job counseling authorities. In a sense, this self-analysis in written form could serve as a valuable source for establishing goals for those first entering the workforce or planning to switch careers. Time permitting, it is worth the effort.

INTERVIEW
QUESTIONS

I attended college but did not graduate because my money ran out. In an interview should I talk about it?

No need to. If the question of college comes up, mention that you attended such and such a college, but unless asked directly, don't go on to explain why you never matriculated. If asked, tell the facts as they are.

Is the interviewer within his rights to ask the applicant what organizations or societies he's affiliated with?

Yes, only if they relate to the applicant's profession or occupation. Beyond that, he could leave himself open to charges of invasion of privacy or discriminatory practices.

When the interviewer says, "Tell me about yourself," where do I begin?

Don't begin from the beginning. He's not interested in how much you weighed when you were born, or your early school years, or when you got your first haircut. This question is merely an icebreaker to get the interview going. Don't bore him with details.

An appropriate reply to a question of this kind is to briefly touch upon your capabilities, strengths, why you want to work for the company, and especially what you can contribute to the company based on your experience. If you have prepared an answer in advance (as you should), your reply need take no more than a minute or so.

If the interviewer wants me to leave my portfolio of samples with him so that he can pass it around to others on the staff, should I comply?

Absolutely not! For several reasons: First, it leaves you without your portfolio to show to other prospects. Then too, there is always the chance that the contents may be soiled in handling, or the entire portfolio go astray. (It occasionally happens.) If he evinces a special interest in one or more samples, you can accommodate him by seeing to it that he gets photocopies. Never part with the originals!

At some point in the interview if the question of transportation facilities for getting to work comes up, would it be to my advantage to mention that I could arrange to join a car pool?

No. Seasoned interviewers know well enough that in any car pool one tardy co-rider can hold up the entire group. It's difficult to clock in on time when you have to rely on others for transportation.

PERSONAL
PROBLEMS

The continued inability to locate an executive-level position to replace the one I lost due to a company merger has made me unsure of myself. I feel that I sometimes act stupid and cause my own failure in job interviews. How can I recoup my selfworth? I still have the ability but I no longer have the confidence.

It's evident that the important position you lost was not due to ineptness but to circumstances beyond your control. Establish contact with a reputable career consultant to get you back on your feet, or join any of the job clubs.

Why is it that when comparing myself with the competition for the job, I find myself inadequate and act that way in the interview—always with negative results?

Your failure to come across in the interview is a self-fulfilling prophecy. If you think that way about yourself, the thought is projected on a wide, 180° screen. No matter how many applicants there are for the job, regard yourself as someone special and bring to light the true qualifications that will overshadow the competition.

I goofed off during my college days and as a consequence piled up some poor grades. Could a prospective employer secure a transcript of my school records by contacting the college?

There's not much fear of that. Student records are considered inviolate and confidential. If your grades have indeed been below par, you would be guilty of falsifying facts if you claimed otherwise. But at the same time there's nothing to be gained by voluntarily disclosing your poor scholastic record when being interviewed.

I can't seem to remember people's names no matter how much I try. When introduced to someone I never met before, I make an effort to fix the name in my mind, but forget it soon after. Can this failing be corrected?

One good way: When you hear a person's name for the first time, ask him how to pronounce it and try to relate his name to some physical aspect of his appearance. But be careful. Don't let that mental association lead you off track. If his name happens to be Mr. Bridget and he is 5'2'', don't inadvertently call him Mr. Midget; if his name is Mr. Obermyer and he has a prominent nose, don't make the mistake of calling him Mr. Obernoser. There are several good books available on memory improvement. I am sure your library has one.

Whenever I am interviewed for a job, I am uneasy in the thought that my hearing aid will be noticed. Shall I do without it since my hearing is only partially impaired? A woman can more easily conceal her hearing aid with a slight modification in hairdo. I can't.

Keep it on with batteries fully charged. You'd feel far more uneasy if you encountered difficulty in understanding what the interviewer is saying, and as a consequence had to occasionally cup your ear or ask him to repeat every so often. One should be no more self-conscious about wearing a hearing aid than wearing eyeglasses. Modern technology has reduced hearing aids to miniscule size, matchable to the color of your skin.

In the interview should I mention my recent divorce?

No, unless the interviewer mentions his, which puts you on common ground. Misery loves company.

Several years ago I suffered a nervous breakdown which required me to be under a doctor's care for some six months. Should I let my interviewer know about this?

No. If he had at one time gone through a nervous breakdown himself, would he tell you about it? Don't mention it unless it comes up in a discussion as a direct question.

My pregnancy still doesn't show. Should I make mention of my condition during the interview?

No, unless the job you are being considered for entails heavy lifting or other strenuous manual labor. Don't prematurely start wearing that nice maternity dress you just added to your wardrobe.

I am a homosexual and not ashamed of it. Would it hurt my chances for getting the job if I alluded to this during the course of the interview?

On the surface, no, but you can never tell what the interviewer's biases are on that subject. No seasoned interviewer will ever inquire about your sexual preferences, nor should you volunteer any such information about this intimate phase of your life.

INTERVIEW
STRATEGY

If you've gotten a number of job offers with other companies, should you mention it to the person interviewing you?

You may do so, but don't appear to give the interviewer the old squeeze-play to force his hand. You can put it this way: "It may interest you to know, Mr._____, that I have gotten several other job offers. I feel, however, I'd be happiest working for your company where I could do the most good with the qualifications I have. I'll get back to you in a few days."

In preparing for an interview, is it necessary for the job applicant to fortify himself with a sales pitch?

It's absolutely necessary, but don't make your presentation sound like a tape recording. The more you can make your sales pitch appear extemporaneous, the more convincing it will be. Mark Twain once said, "The best speech I ever made extemporaneously took me two weeks to prepare.''

If the interview is going my way, is it good strategy for me to ask for the job, or is it better to wait for the prospective employer to make the offer?

If you feel you've made a good impression, strike while the iron is hot. Definitely ask for the job even though you aren't sure you're ready to sign up on the spot. Remember, in an extended job-search campaign, the more offers you have, the greater are the number of options at your disposal.

What's the cause of pre-interview sickness which I experience whenever I apply for a job?

Most likely lack of self-confidence due to inadequate preparation. See what a difference it makes when you do your homework!

How do you turn down a job offer that looks good but you're not sure that it's the one for you?

Thank the interviewer. Let him know that you are flattered by the offer, but say you have several other prospects you want to check out before making a commitment. Leave the door open.

What's the best time of day for a job interview?

Late afternoon, when the interviewer has mentally cancelled out other candidates he's seen so far. Mornings and early afternoons the interviewer is inclined to be feisty and particular. As the day wears on, he lets down a little and becomes less choosy. Generally, he remembers best the person he's interviewed last. In a study by Robert Half, head of one of the largest recruiting networks in the world, it was found that the last in a string of applicants interviewed in any one day is three times more likely to be hired than those who preceded him. The person first interviewed is not paid much attention, and usually does not get the job offer.

If the interview started late or was extended, and I have another one lined up to go to without further delay, should I explain the situation to the interviewer?

Don't hesitate to do so; he'll understand. In the future, avoid scheduling your interviews too close to each other to cause you undue stress.

If at the end of the interview session, the interviewer says, "Thanks for dropping in. I enjoyed our little chat." What does that mean?

It means you are not the one, or he has no job open—and if he had, you still are not the one. If he adds, "good luck," then you can be sure he won't be your next employer. Look elsewhere.

Is it alright to accompany my daughter, a recent high school graduate, to her first job interview?

If she's old enough to pay full fare, she's old enough to go to an interview on her own without a chaperone.

On a number of occasions, the person interviewing me was called out of the office for what seemed to be a long five minutes, leaving me to myself. What is one to do under such circumstances?

Well, here's what you should *NOT* do. You should not yield to the impulse to handle anything on the interviewer's desk. Instead, use the time to good advantage by looking over your resume and other credentials. Trade secret: It is not rare for an interviewer to absent himself from the office intentionally, leaving the door slightly ajar, so that the candidate's action and behavior can be observed unbeknownst to him during that unguarded interlude.

I've heard it said that when the chair intended for the interviewee to sit on is placed in a certain position, it's best not to move it about. Is that correct?

If the chair is not nailed down to the floor, there's no reason why you shouldn't move it to where you're most comfortable—but not too close to the desk, nor so far away where you and the interviewer will have to talk a few decibels higher to hear each other. Take a middle distance. However, when the interview is over, remember to replace the chair to its original position. You can be sure your interviewer will take notice of this and it will be in your favor.

EMPLOYMENT AGENCIES, COUNSELORS, AND RECRUITERS

If an employment agency ad states, "fee paid," who is it that pays the fee, the applicant or the would-be employer?

Admittedly, the phrase "fee paid" is ambiguous. However, through common usage it has gotten to mean that it is the employer who pays the agency fee, *not* the applicant.

I am more than six years out of school and at present unemployed. Would it be productive for me to visit the placement office of my alma mater to talk to the counselor about a job?

You can lose nothing by it—only gain. It could very well be that the placement counselor has on file a backlog of employers seeking former students with the kind of work experience you have acquired since you were graduated. In addition, you may get the opportunity to renew your acquaintance with former instructors. Perhaps one or more may be in a position to help you get placed. Often, seeking advice or assistance from anyone is a form of compliment. Then too, while there, you can find out when the next alumni get-together is scheduled so that you will be able to meet and mingle with class chums who could be instrumental in suggesting a lead to a job or even arrange an interview for you.

In what way does a part-time employee differ from a "temp?"

The part-time employee is on the payroll of one particular company on a steady basis and is for all practical purposes considered a permanent member of the regular work force. The temp, on the other hand, is basically a freelancer, "rented out" as it were, to a client company on a contractual basis by an agency who has made a specialty of temporary employment.

I tried to locate executive search firms which I know exist but for some reason don't show the address in phone directories. What's the reason for that?

Busy executive recruiters want to head off a barrage of unemployed job seekers from coming in uninvited. According to the *Fordyce Letter,* a publication for employment professionals, many recruiters complain that it takes too much time to interview unlikely prospects who drop in without a previous appointment.

As a general policy, do campus recruiters hire only straight A students? I am not one of them.

Not always. While recruiters will pass up students with below-average scholastic records, they will give due consideration to those who impress them with their personality and evince a strong desire to succeed on the job. They also know from experience that straight A students tend to overestimate their true worth, demanding starting salaries way above the prevalent scale for entry jobs.

Is there a basis in truth that anyone who has spent a good part of his work life in Civil Service or in the Military is not looked upon with favor—or to put it more boldly, is often discriminated against when applying for a job in the private sector? If this is so, what is one to do under the circumstances?

Unfortunately, this describes the situation quite accurately. In the world of business anyone with that work background represents a stereotype of an individual lacking in self-direction and ambition, is unthinking, and is apt to goof off on the job.

In answer to the second question: When composing a resume, develop it on a functional rather than a chronological format, thus calling less attention to the years of actual service. At the interview, relate how the particular skills and knowledge acquired in the service are transferable and bear a direct relationship to the requirements of the job under discussion. Change an apparent liability into a positive asset.

In the last five years, I've been temporarily laid off or permanently displaced from four different jobs due to company mergers, changeovers in administration, etc.— and I'm tired of it. For that reason I'm looking for a career in Civil Service which promises greater job security. Where can I get detailed information about opportunities in Civil Service?

There are a number of sources:

1. Get in touch with the various Departments of Personnel directly, or any one of the regional federal Offices of Personnel Management.

2. Contact Simon & Schuster's Reference Group (Prentice Hall Press) in New York, publishers of a special line of guidebooks in various branches of government work—local, state, and federal. In addition to general information about government employment, Arco Civil Service Test Tutors books feature previous written exams and corresponding answers.

3. Subscribe to *The Chief*, one of several newspapers devoted exclusively to current news and job openings in government work.

4. Ask your librarian for newsletters and other printed matter periodically distributed to libraries by the Personnel Departments of various government agencies.

5. Specific information on federal jobs is available by subscription to Federal Jobs Digest NE, 325 Pennsylvania Ave., S.E., Washington, DC 20003.

I've always wanted to put in some time working overseas for an American company. What are my prospects?

Better than it used to be, but still rather slim. Job opportunities abroad are not quite as numerous or as glamorous as is commonly believed. While it's true that salaries are high, so is the cost of living. Generally speaking, most firms are reluctant to place newcomers in overseas assignments. Then too, except for key personnel and highly skilled technicians, the prevailing practice is to employ local help wherever possible.

Although at this writing there are approximately 1.8 million Americans living and working abroad, many of them are self-employed, adventurous entrepreneurs who like the idea of living abroad.

If I want to find out more about overseas job openings that do exist, how do I go about it?

Directories listing American firms with overseas branches are available in most libraries. In addition, there are a number of guidebooks on overseas jobs, among them Juvenal Angel's *A Select Guide to Overseas Employment*, Curtis Casewit's *How to Get a Job Overseas* and his *Overseas Jobs in the Private Sector and Government Employment*.

Detailed information on job openings abroad can be gotten by contacting Employment International, P.O. Box 19760, Indianapolis, IN 46219. This is not an employment agency; it is strictly a commercial guidance organization for those seeking overseas jobs.

JOB APPLICATIONS

Should a physical handicap be noted on job applications?

No need to mention it at this time. Write *none* in the space allotted to this question. Assuming that you are technically qualified for the job in all respects, you are in fact not handicapped.

In the event that the subject of your physical disability comes up on a personal interview—as it might—you can explain that it has not proven to be a hindrance to your performance on the job in the past and is not likely to do so in the future.

When asked to fill out a job application, is it better to do so right then and there, or take it with you to fill out at home?

Where feasible, take it with you. In the leisurely ambience of your home, you'll be less tense and consequently do a more creditable job in both accuracy of information and neatness. As an added advantage, you'll have the opportunity to photocopy the completely filled-in application for your own records and followup purposes.

As a walk-in job seeker or one applying for an advertised position, does a firm have a right to refuse to let me have a job application blank?

Legally, no. If the firm has applications on hand, you cannot be denied one whether or not you appear to be the kind of person they would consider hiring.

In addressing a letter to a firm when you don't know the name of the principal you wish to reach, is the proper salutation "To Whom It May Concern," or "Dear Sir or Madam?"

Neither. If you don't know the name, it's easy enough to find out by phoning the company. It's just short of a personal insult to be the recipient of any correspondence addressed that way. It's only one step away from receiving junk mail addressed to "Dear Occupant."

It is known that mail addressed to an executive officer of a large corporation is initially reviewed by his secretary. How can I get around this to be sure that my correspondence is not intercepted by an intermediary?

A gambit that sometimes works is to mark the envelope *Personal* or *Confidential*.

When I require a limited number of resumes, just enough to send off to a few job prospects, is it okay to send carbon copies to avoid the expense of having them reproduced by a commercial printer?

It would be foolish to make carbon copies when for pennies you can get perfect duplicates of your master resume reproduced by the Xerox or similar photocopying method. No prospective employer would for one moment consider an applicant who doesn't have more sense than to send a carbon copy of a resume.

Would you send off a carbon copy of a love letter to your best boy or girlfriend?

So many people compliment me on the quality of my penmanship. Do you think a prospective employer would pay special attention to my resume if I were to write it by hand?

It all depends. If you are rightfully proud of your calligraphic penmanship, such a resume will certainly get noticed.

There are instances where firms actually request job applicants to submit a handwritten resume when the nature of the job calls for a special ability to write clearly and neatly. Apart from this, there may be an entirely different reason for asking for handwritten resumes—

namely, to get an analytical evaluation of a prospective employee's character and personality traits by a professional graphologist who works hand-in-hand with the Personnel Department. To the discerning eye of a graphologist, handwriting can reveal a lot about the writer's temperament, native intelligence, dexterity, creativity, honesty, and aggressiveness. Some graphologists go as far as to claim that handwriting can also reveal height, weight, age, even sexual preference—though this is disputable.

In Japan and some European countries an analysis of a candidate's handwriting is a common procedure in the hiring process.

How can I make my resume different without resorting to stunts or gimmicks, so it won't get lost in the haystack of resumes that reach the interviewer's desk?

If it's brief, neat, and to the point, that will make it "different" enough. However, to introduce a personal touch, consider one of the following suggestions: jot down a few cogent remarks in the margin; highlight certain statements with a transparent color marker; hand-sign each copy of the resume with a felt-tip pen.

I have not had any formal education to speak of. Should I omit the Educational Background *heading in my resume?*

It would seem a mistake in judgment to do so simply because you have no degree or diploma. Mention any specific training programs you have successfully completed, technical seminars you attended, correspondence courses you may have taken, or other evidence of self-improvement. Any effort in that direction often makes a favorable impression on a prospective employer. Make the most of what you have.

How long should it take to complete a perfect resume?

No resume is "perfect," but you should try to come close to it. A full day would not be too long. Putting together a resume calls for a lot of thinking, writing, and numerous revisions to get all the information down to fit one or two pages, and that cannot be rushed.

I've endeavored to prepare my own resume (as I know I should), but the results are not successful. The several professional resume writers I went to quoted fees beyond my means, since my only income at present is the unemployment benefits I get. What can I do?

If you can't manage to prepare a good resume through your own efforts, get some knowledgeable friend to help you, or contact the SES or local "Y" for assistance. Also, there is no shortage of inexpensive paperbacks on the subject which you can either buy or borrow from your library to guide you. When you run out of money, you have to use your brains.

I am realistic enough to know that many unsolicited resumes are often not read or even looked at. How can I at least make sure that the resume I send out reaches its destination?

Invest in extra postage and send it registered mail with return receipt requested. In a week or so, if you don't get a signed receipt, follow up with a phone call. Incidentally, this will also give you an opportunity to identify yourself on a personal basis.

Is it true that a resume set up in printer's type is usually more effective than one reproduced from typewritten copy?

Not always. A typeset resume, though perhaps more professional in appearance, can miss its mark. The trouble with a typeset resume is that it may just look *too* professional, giving the distinct impression that it has been designed commercially for mass distribution.

Should a Social Security number appear on a resume?

Not necessarily. However, this information is usually called for on a job application form, and, of course, you'll need it when you are put on the payroll.

What can a recent college graduate such as myself submit as evidence of work experience when in fact I don't have any?

Yes, you do. Think back. Did you at one time or other serve as camp counselor or lifeguard? Have you ever had a paper route; mowed lawns for neighbors on a pay basis; helped with charity drives; assisted in local political campaigns; did tutoring? Anything else like that? Not all need be full-time salaried positions, but they all constitute work experience.

Does anyone ever read a three-page resume?

The person interviewing a candidate for a high-level managerial or executive position will go through a three-page resume if it is well organized. Generally speaking, a one-page resume is preferred, two pages are acceptable. Beyond that, you risk the chance that your resume will end up in the recycling machine, unread.

POLYGRAPH
& APTITUDE
TESTS

How truthful are the polygraph tests used in screening job applicants?

The results of the test must be analyzed by a human being and therein lies room for human error. It is possible for a person to honestly answer questions which can be interpreted as untrue, and at the same time it is possible for a person to lie and fool the polygraph and the tester.

How do polygraphs work?

The polygraph is based on the principle that when a person tells an untruth in answer to a question, his emotional responses manifest themselves in a sudden rise in blood pressure and heightened perspiration and breathing rates. These are graphically recorded, analyzed by experts and end up in the form of a printout of the findings.

I find being asked to take a polygraph test personally demeaning. Does the interviewer have the legal right to make it a contingency for employment?

Yes, in most states he does, if the nature of the job applied for warrants it as a screening device and the test is applied in an objective, non-discriminatory manner.

Frankly speaking, how accurate are aptitude and psychological tests for predicting success in a given career?

The most cogent statement on the subject comes from a highly qualified and outspoken psychologist who is quoted as saying, ''After all is said and done, the most direct way to predict anybody's success in a career is to simply ask, 'What would you like to do?' ''
It's always difficult to make predictions, especially about the future.

ARRIVING TO
INTERVIEW
WITH TIME
TO SPARE

Should it turn out that I reach the location where the interview is to take place considerably sooner than planned, and as a result find I have lots of time at my disposal, what do I do under the circumstances?

Well, here's what you should *not* do. Don't make your appearance more than a scant five minutes before post-time set for the interview.

Four suggestions come to mind whereby you can put that extra time to best use.

1. Survey the general neighborhood. Are there good schools for the kids, places of worship? What about cultural facilities, shopping, parking, good restaurants? In sum, is this the kind of socio-economic milieu that you and your family would be comfortable in, should relocation be advisable?

2. Visit the company cafeteria. Nearly all large firms have in-house cafeterias open during business hours for coffee breaks and lunch. Stop in for a snack and don't hesitate joining a table where others are seated. Keep your ears open for any shoptalk (yes, even gossip!) which may clue you in on some aspects of the company that could be of particular interest to you as a future employee. From what you observe around you, what appears to be the general morale of the staff? Are your prospective co-workers friendly and affable, the kind you would like to work with?

3. Consider contacting other firms in the building: Time permitting, scan the lobby directory for names of firms in your line of work with the idea of dropping in to see them after your interview, on a cold-turkey basis. By doing so, you will have several built-in advantages in your favor. You are dressed for the occasion, you have the necessary credentials on hand, and you need not lose precious time traveling all over town. By sheer coincidence you could be the Johnny-on-the-spot the firm has been looking for, having come by at the right time, to the right place for a job that you never hoped to land so easily.

4. Visit the restroom for a last-minute check on your appearance. Is your hair still neatly arranged as when you started out? Does your makeup need touching up? And at the risk of being personal, I suggest that you stop over at the john (or jane) before your scheduled interview. Remember, there are no "restroom breaks" during the interview.

ABOUT
WANT-ADS

In the last six weeks I've mailed more than 60 letters of application and resumes in response to want ads. Results: no invitations to interviews, no outright rejections, not even "we'll keep your resume on file." Should I continue?

What else do you plan to do, or is this what you call a total job-search campaign?

What is the distinction between a classified ad and a display ad?

A classified ad is generally smaller in size and, while it can vary in length, it is confined to the width of a newspaper column. The wording is printed in a limited number of standard typefaces. Billing is computed by the number of lines of type matter it takes. A display ad, on the other hand, can be made any size and dimensions, with any choice of typefaces, border designs, and other decorative elements. Such an ad is prepared by the newspaper's own art department or by an outside advertising agency. Because of higher costs, display ads are generally placed by firms, whereas classified ads are placed by individuals.

Should "salary required" (if asked for in an ad) be stated in the reply?

No, never directly. Disregard it entirely or say, "salary to be discussed in interview." An alternative is to give a salary range. At no time, however, name a definite salary prior to the interview.

In answering an ad calling for a skill in which I happen to excel, would it help my cause to say that I can handle just about anything in my line of work?

It could do you more harm than good. If the employer is looking for someone with a specific skill, he is not interested in a jack-of-all-trades. Versatility is sometimes defined as being mediocre in many things.

I've heard it said that firms that run blind ads often have no existing openings. Then why do they advertise?

There are two possible explanations. One is to check out the available labor supply in their line of work; the other is to surreptitiously find out who among their employees are playing the field, totally unaware that they are replying to the very company they are working for. To quote a famous line in the movie *Casablanca*, "round up the usual suspects."

Is there an advantage to be among the first to reply to a want ad?

One would normally think so, but it doesn't always work out that way. An attractive job opening can pull in hundreds of replies, all coming in about the same time. Strategically, it is sometimes better to let a few days go by before mailing in yours. In that way, your letter of application is less likely to be lost in a stack of those of your competitors.

I read of one applicant who capitalized on his late reply by writing, "Dear Director of Personnel, now that you heard from the others and had a chance to review their resumes, I'd like you to consider mine, herewith enclosed. I believe you'll find my qualifications special." A novel approach of this kind will certainly not fail to get individual attention, and may earn you an invitation to an interview.

Why don't box number advertisers show the courtesy to answer those who take the trouble to reply?

It's mostly a matter of economics. When the advertiser receives a heavy turnout of responses, it's too costly in clerical time and postage to reply to each applicant. You may be sure that if a firm is interested in you, you will be contacted. In the meantime, on with the job hunt!

JOB CLUBS

Though I have much to say, I am shy by nature, and lack the confidence to express myself—especially in an interview situation. How can I overcome this handicap without committing myself to an expensive, long-range program?

Perhaps your best bet is to join one of the Toastmasters' clubs in your community. Toastmasters is a world-wide, non-profit organization with more than 4500 chapters offering ongoing programs for those wishing to develop confidence as well as the ability to speak convincingly. The program is not conducted like a course with an academic setting, but more like a practical workshop. Clubs meet in informal sessions at various hours of the day or evening, and membership dues are very nominal. For the chapter nearest you, consult your local phone book, or else write to the home office, Toastmasters Int'l, P.O. Box 10400, Santa Ana, CA 92711.

An executive out of a job at 46, I am too old for a paper route and too young for Social Security. I find my age against me when contacting job prospects. To whom can I turn for the guidance I so sorely need without spending thousands of dollars in professional fees at a time when I can least afford it?

Assuming your former company does not have an ongoing outplacement program, here is a suggestion you may want to consider. Join a mutual-help group such as the Forty Plus club, whose objective is not merely to lend psychological support to displaced executives like yourself (as important as that is) but to provide practical down-to-earth assistance in honing up on resume preparation, writing letters of application, practicing interviewing, and related skills. For particulars about location and membership requirements contact the Office of the President, Forty Plus of New York, 15 Park Row, New York, NY 10038.

Among other sources of assistance you should make an effort to explore, are the Man Marketing Council, Sales Executive Club, Advertising Club of New York, as well as schools and universities offering career seminars on a nominal fee basis. You'll find most sources listed in the Calendar of Events page of the *National Business Employment Weekly,* published by Dow Jones & Company, Inc., 420 Lexington Ave., New York, NY 10170.

HIDDEN JOB MARKET

What impression would I, as a job seeker, convey when contacting a prospective employer without previous arrangement—cold turkey style?

It's hard to tell. That would depend upon your approach as well as the type of person he is. In most cases, you can assume that he would be favorably impressed with your spunk; it would show you to be a go-getter, enterprising, and ambitious—qualities that are looked for in any employee, particularly in sales. You must be ready for many rejections, many no's, but all you need is just one *yes.*

I recently lost my job and frankly I'm embarrassed about it. Should I confide in my relatives and friends?

If your house were on fire, would you keep it a secret and not call the fire department? By all means, let it be known to one and all that you're out of a job. Brief them about your qualifications and the type of job you are looking for. Hand out resumes unstintingly. Someone among them may give you a lead, or know someone else who can. The more you make your availability known, the better your chances for landing the job you want.

In phone solicitation, what part of the day is it best to call and reach the hiring executive without interception by a secretary?

Most people think early mornings are best. Not always so. Try after 5 o'clock, when the company switchboard may still be open, but the secretary has left for the day and the executive is the one to pick up the phone.

Is it wrong to ask a third party to arrange a job interview for me?

No, if the third party and your prospective employer happen to be buddy-buddies or long-time business associates. If that is the case, your ''sponsor'' can be materially helpful in arranging an interview for you on a person-to-person basis.

In answering an advertised job opening or when making a cold-turkey call via the phone, should I discuss my background to show how qualified I am for the job?

Briefly allude to select highlights of your work experience but don't go into great detail. Another thing—don't allow yourself to be interviewed on the phone, sight unseen. All you are interested in now is to arrange for an interview. At no time keep the prospective employer on the phone for more than two or three minutes.

ABOUT JOB
DISCRIMINATION

What phase of job discrimination is most prevalent?

Age discrimination still ranks first, followed by race, sex, national origin, and religion. We have as yet a long way to go to eliminate job discrimination in all its ugly phases.

Occasionally I come across the term, "protected classes." Just what does it mean?

This is an umbrella term used to identify segments of the working force commonly subject to discriminatory labor practices because of their ethnic background, sex, age, color of skin, or physical handicap.

I was a loyal and dedicated employee with one company for practically all my working life, eventually reaching the level of Director of Product Marketing.
On my 60th birthday (which incidentally coincided with the 35th year of my joining the company) I was called in on Thursday to the office of a new executive who moved in from a company that bought us out. Instead of being congratulated as I fully expected to be on this dual event in my life, this fellow, 25 years my junior, let me know that my services would no longer be required starting next Monday. There were no complaints as to my performance on the job or anything else, except I was no longer needed. My whole life collapsed around me. At 60, where could I find a job with a salary equal to that I was making? Who needs a has-been when younger people are available with much lower salary expectations? From a somebody, I became a nobody.
What course of action is left open for a person in my situation?

There is no doubt that you have a serious problem—that is, your age. Unless you are prepared, or desperate enough to take a substantial drop in salary (even if you could get any reasonable job offer at this time of life), do what excessed executives and retired persons have found to be expedient. Make a concerted effort to sell your services as a consultant in the field of your expertise. In this capacity you may earn as much, if not more, than a salaried employee and enjoy a professional status commensurate with your experience. Contact new companies in your field who are setting up in business or those long established who have a technical problem in which your expertise can be the solution. This is a common practice in many professions and occupations—law, engineering, accountancy, business management, the graphic arts.

In essence, you are starting a new career, yet you remain in the field in which you can be considered an expert. Consultants don't work on a fixed salary; they are not on the company payroll. They work on a professional fee basis which not infrequently yields higher annual earnings than a regular employee punching the clock.

There are a number of helpful books which tell the would-be consultant how to get started, ways to build up a clientele, how to figure fees, etc. Among the more recent is *How to Become a Successful Consultant in Your Own Field* by Hubert Bermont, an acknowledged authority on the subject. For information contact: Consultant's Library, Dept. BEW 19, 815 Fifteenth St., N.W., Washington, DC 20005.

With a name like Hilda Abramowitz I find it a vexing problem to get a foot in the door for a key position in banking, though I come highly qualified. I strongly suspect that my ethnic-sounding name has something to do with it. As a matter of expediency should I use an assumed name for job procurement purposes?

Unquestionably, in certain businesses, such as banking, engineering, and the aerospace industries, there is still a lingering bias against hiring ethnic groups for key positions. It will take a bit of time for this to totally disappear. Resorting to a fictitious name has a somewhat fraudulent ring to it and can lead to unforeseen complications. If you can't wait for this bias to disappear completely, consider a legal name change, a course adopted by so many others for one reason or another.

I read somewhere that 40% of all interviewers are said to be biased and prejudiced. What about the others?

The others don't admit it.

What (if any) penalties face employers guilty of job discrimination in hiring or promotional practices?

In most instances not enough to scare them. A firm doing business with the government will be denied the privilege to bid on any government contracts in the future. However, there are cases on record of class action suits brought against firms for engaging in discriminatory practices in hiring and promotion, where millions of dollars in back pay were awarded to groups of people who successfully proved that they were discriminated against because of age, religion, or ethnic background.

Occasionally I come across questions on job application forms asking for marital status, place and date of birth, sex, number and ages of dependents, incidents of arrests, etc.—all of which, to my knowledge, have long been considered to be discriminatory in nature. Why in this day and age do questions such as these still appear on some applications?

For a number of reasons. In some instances the job application forms were devised by employers who are still unaware that questions like these are off limits. And then, there are those employers who knowingly and deliberately are guilty of discriminatory practices. Another possible explanation is that a firm's supply of applications have not as yet been updated.

Whatever the case may be, you are within your rights to ignore questions that you deem to be discriminatory in nature.

PROBLEM INTERVIEWERS

What do you make of the following situation? An interviewer presents a glowing scenario of the future that awaits me as a company employee, without seeming to pay much attention to my qualifications for the job.

He is gilding the lily and his sales pitch should be looked upon with suspicion. Do further research on both the reputation of the company as well as the integrity of the interviewer. When offered two dimes for a nickel, always test the coins.

I listen when the interviewer is talking, but the trouble is he doesn't listen to me. I have the feeling I'm talking to a blank wall for all the feedback I get. Who is at fault, he or I?

Maybe both. It could very well be that the interviewer at the moment has other things on his mind (personal or otherwise) which in effect block out what you're saying. Then too, it could be you, in that your voice lacks animation and that you don't show sufficient enthusiasm in your general approach to arouse his interest.

I am aware that for certain customer-service and other public-contact positions, it is not unusual for the interviewer to rough you up a bit to see how you would react under job stress. What do you say or do, however, when the position you're applying for is not particularly stress-oriented and the hostile behavior of the interviewer seems due more to a perversity of character than to anything else?

You can say something like this: "Mr. Employer, I believe I am not obliged to tolerate this type of interview treatment which I find offensive and I am certain you would feel the same way if we changed places."

If he persists in this mode of conduct, however, politely beg to be excused. Head for the nearest exit, but don't slam the door on your way out. For all you know, realizing his indiscretion, he may call you back and take a more conciliatory approach to the interview process. And what's more, he might even compliment you for your spunk.

How can I disengage myself from an interviewer who keeps chatting on and on, and it looks as if the interview is going nowhere with no job offer in sight?

If you feel you've said all you want to say and so has he (of any importance to you), and it becomes obvious that he just likes to talk, glance at your watch and remark that you've enjoyed meeting with him but you have another engagement to attend. Exit gracefully. Upon leaving the office, mark him down in your little notebook as a ''nudnik'' and cross him off your list of prospects.

SEXUAL
INNUENDOS

If you are applying for a job as personal secretary and your would-be boss hints that his wife doesn't understand him, is he trying to tell you something?

Quite possibly he's looking for an office wife and all that it entails. Then too, there's more than one executive I've come across who complains to his wife that his *secretary* doesn't understand him.

How serious is the problem of sexual harassment when being interviewed for a job or seeking a promotion?

Serious enough for any man or woman to be alerted to it in the job market.

Why is it that interviewers frequently try to make a pass at me as if that were standard procedure in the interview process?

It could be that innocently enough your mode of dress and coquettish behavior flash signals.

RAPPORT
WITH
INTERVIEWERS

You say, ''If you want the interviewer to like you, you must like him.'' Supposing I don't like him. What then?

Every human being (yes, even a job interviewer) possesses redeeming qualities. Look for them in the person interviewing you and they are bound to emerge as you get to know him a little better.

I'd feel more comfortable if the interviewer and I were on a first name basis. How can I bring this about?

One way is to follow a course something like this: When introducing yourself (using my own name as an example), say, ''My name is Biegeleisen.'' Pause for a moment, then say, ''*Jack* Biegeleisen,'' placing emphasis on the first name. This should give the interviewer a hint to follow suit.

In anticipation of shaking hands with an interviewer, my hand gets clammy cold. I know it makes a bad impression, but what I don't know is what to do about it.

Before meeting him, it sometimes helps to place your hand on the side of your neck for a moment or two. You'll find that this will not only warm your hand but reduce the clamminess as well. Try it.

SALARY
BENEFITS &
PERKS

A prospective employer flatly turns down my salary request with, "I'm sorry, I can't offer you any more." How do I proceed at this point?

For one thing, don't cut off further negotiations right then and there. If you can't shake the money tree any more in terms of base salary, and your heart is set on the job, try for additional benefits and perks—among them, more frequent salary reviews, bonuses, choice of insurance plans, or company-subsidized training programs.

In considering a salary offer do you see anything wrong in saying, "I'd like to consult my husband (wife) before making a decision to accept?"

Sounds like the right thing to do, doesn't it? But I wouldn't recommend it. This may plant a doubt in the interviewer's mind that you lack the confidence to come to a decision on your own—a serious drawback in some job situations.

What's the distinction between fringe benefits and perks?

All employees of a company are entitled to standard fringe benefits set up by the company, across the board. Perks, however, are offered on a discretionary basis to a select few employees only.

How much severance pay does the average company provide employees who are let go?

This depends on individual company-employee agreements that contain stipulations on that score. The amount may vary anywhere from two weeks to six months or even a year's salary. If a company wants to push out a high-ranking executive, part of the inducement may be an attractive severance allowance to buy up his contract.

How binding is a verbal agreement governing such matters as salary, bonuses, severance pay, and other fringe benefits and perks?

Samuel Goldwyn, the one-time movie magnate, was once quoted as saying, "A verbal agreement is not worth the paper it's written on." He was not exactly right about that. The fact is that any agreement—verbal or otherwise—made by two parties in good faith can be legally binding. Even a mere handshake to finalize an understanding could be considered as a legal agreement and upheld as such in a court of law. That in fact is the form of "contract" widely adopted in New York City's bustling jewelry exchange where business transactions involving hundreds of thousands of dollars are confirmed by nothing more than a handshake followed by the Hebrew expression, "Mazel 'n Bruche," which translated means, "Luck and Blessings."

All said and done, it's always easier to prove your case when you have on hand a legally drawn contract in which all the facts and conditions are clearly spelled out in black and white.

I occasionally come across the term "cafeteria-style" benefits. What does it mean?

It refers to the option a company offers its employees to select from among a varied menu of benefits those that best reflect their personal circumstances and needs. This applies to such matters as the type of medical coverage and dental insurance, subsidized tuition for self and family, choice of retirement plans, and so on.

An example: An employee who already has sufficient medical coverage might select added vacation time instead, or he may decide to forfeit his vacation and stay on the job for the extra money. In essence the employee doesn't surrender any of his benefits, but he's given the privilege to opt for others in exchange.

Is there an advantage in asking for a contract as part of the total money package?

Not always. While a contract protects your rights and obviously has its good points, it can become a millstone around your neck. If the job doesn't work out right, you may be restricted from tying up with another company until the termination date of the contract, and sometimes several years after it. What's more, if the company wants to get rid of you, it can directly or otherwise make your continued stay so miserable that you are the one to break the contract and face whatever penalties that go with such a move.

Is there a law making it mandatory for a company to provide pension plans for its employees? If so, are all employees unilaterally covered by it?

No, to both questions.

There is no law on the books compelling a company to provide a pension plan for its employees. And if there is a pension plan, it doesn't necessarily follow that all employees of the company are included.

Legally, a new employee has the right to a clear understanding of a company's pension plans and how he is affected by it. Many large companies have this information available in printed form; with others you have to make personal inquiries about it.

For a full understanding of what your rights are in the matter of company pension plans, contact the area office of the U.S. Department of Labor, or write to Pension Publications, 1346 Connecticut Ave., N.W., Washington, DC 20036, for their, "Guide to Understanding Your Pension Plans."

What happens when a high-level executive joins a company late in his career and does not have time to build up accrued benefits towards his retirement?

The firm can make up for this by providing supplementary plans in computing his retirement pay. This, however, is more a matter of personal negotiation than standard procedure.

ABOUT
REFERENCES

Before giving a former employer's name as reference, how can I be sure in advance whether I'll be damned or praised?

The most direct and best way is to ask him personally. A covert way is to have a friend or associate in business inquire about you on a business letterhead.

What can be done if an ex-boss continues to hex my chances for getting another job by bad-mouthing me whenever he is contacted by a prospective employer?

To take the edge off his residual grievance against you (justifiable or not), drop in to see him, or write him a brief note. Say that you sincerely regret whatever it was that made him feel that way about you, and hope he will realize the harm this is causing you in getting a job elsewhere. Very likely you'll find his attitude towards you will soften, thus getting the monkey off your back once and for all.

In instances where malice without due cause is intended, you can institute legal action against him for defamation of character.

Is the interviewer within his rights to contact my present or former employers if I do not list them as references on my resume or job application?

There is nothing to stop him. He is not violating any ethical or legal code by contacting any employer, whether listed or not, as references. This is part of the investigative procedure in screening applicants. If, however, you have a gentleman's agreement with him to desist from contacting your present employer who you do not wish to know that you are contemplating a job switch, then you would expect the interviewer to abide by that agreement until you are offered the job.

My previous employer said he'd be glad to give me a letter of recommendation but at the moment is just too pressed for time to do it. (Incidentally, from what I know about him, he is not adept at composing letters of this type—or any other type—whether he has the time or not.) Do you think it would be alright for me to draft such a letter for him in view of the fact that he is "too busy" to take care of it himself?

This expediency is nothing new. It has been resorted to many times. I suggest that you put it to him this way:
"Mr. _____, realizing your busy work schedule, I've taken the liberty of preparing a rough draft for you to look over—and of course feel free to make any changes you see fit."
This approach will give him the feeling he's done it himself.

JOB SWITCH

Is it wrong to use my present firm's business stationery for correspondence in planning a job switch?

You are doing nothing wrong as long as you first obtain permission and let your employer know that you're seeking a job change—and you have his blessings. In fact, there can be an advantage in resorting to this. It shows that you are employed at present and, as everybody knows, your chances for getting a job are always better when you already have a job than when you are unemployed.

I deeply regret having impulsively left a good job as Associate Editor for a small but growing company for a Managing Editor's position in a major book publishing house. It turned out for various reasons to be a disaster. What's to be learned from the experience?

If you've made a mistake in judgment don't let regrets rankle in your soul. Follow the example of the great financier and presidential advisor, the late Bernard Baruch. After making a wrong move in the stock market that resulted in serious financial losses, Baruch is quoted as saying, "In similar circumstances some men would grow desperate: I grew cautious. I began a habit I was never to forsake—analyzing my losses to determine where I had made my mistakes. I never sought to excuse myself, but was concerned solely with guarding against a repetition of the same error.''

Next time when you contemplate switching jobs or making any serious career change, weigh your options carefully before you make a move.

What are some of the signals which make an employer suspect that one of his workers is setting his sights to jump ship for another port?

If the employee:

—on some days is spiffed up and better groomed than usual.

—more than once calls in sick or asks for time off during the day for a variety of reasons.

—takes extended lunch hours.

—requests a change from his scheduled vacation time.

—receives and makes a greater number of personal phone calls.

—is observed to be daydreaming and preoccupied with his own thoughts.

—keeps his usually cluttered desk surface clean.

At present I hold down a full-time job and don't have the opportunity during regular business hours to use the phone freely to contact potential employers for a contemplated job change. How would it be for a member of my family or a friend to make these calls for me?

It would be much better if you did your own calling. Perhaps you can manage to do so during coffee breaks and lunch hours. If necessary, take a day off for ''personal reasons'' (even if you are docked for it) to make your phone contacts. With an organized list of prospects on hand, you should be able to put in 15 to 20 calls a day without difficulty.

I've had several interesting job offers recently but can't make up my mind which to accept.

Too much window shopping and you may be left out in the cold. Any job is better than none, only if it is used as a stopgap until the real opportunity you've been waiting for comes along. This, in essence, is the considered opinion of Robert Snelling, a highly reputed authority in the employment field. Other authorities of equal professional status differ strongly on that point. ''Don't accept a stopgap job,'' they warn, ''it may turn out to be a permanent rut.'' I personally concur with the latter opinion.

What am I to do when the job I've held for the past four years has been unful-filling and a big bore. Should I finally throw in the towel and return to the job-hunt trail?

Four years of boredom is long enough, but hold off leaving your present job until another prospect turns up. Your rating with a new employer drops when you are among the unemployed.

I've been a baker for most of my working years—an expert at it—but feel it's time to make a change. As long as I remember, I've always liked animals, especially dogs and, with that in mind, I'm thinking of taking up dog grooming as a career. I've been told there's good money to be made in it. Should I follow through?

Remember, if you get into a new field without transferring the knowledge and experience you've acquired throughout the years, you put yourself to a disadvantage. From an expert in one, you become an amateur in another.

If it's dough you're after, stay in the baking business. Since you claim to be a long-time dog lover, why not develop a cottage-industry business, baking dog biscuits for distribution to retail outlets and in time build up a reputation as the best darn dog biscuit baker in town?

When is it best to look for a job?

When you have one!

If you are out of work and have been for some time, your anxiety mounts with each passing week. This is bound to show up in your approach, your attitude—even in your appearance when being interviewed. You get to think of yourself as a loser and present that image to a prospective employer.

You'll walk straighter and with greater self-assurance when you already have a job but wish to explore the possibilities of switching to another that holds out better prospects.

JOBS FOR THE FUTURE

Just how accurate are the various forecasts I come across which project the high-demand jobs of the future?

About as accurate as the stock market forecasts and a little better than the weather predictions.

To give you an example: Back in 1968 when I was doing research for a forthcoming book on careers and opportunities in teaching, I tapped every source of information—the National Education Association, the United Federation of Teachers, the Bureau of Labor Statistics, and various other government and private agencies—for statistics on the anticipated supply and demand for teaching personnel in the public school system. The unilateral conclusion was that for the next 25 years, the demand for teachers would continue to grow and by far outstrip the supply. No sooner had my book come off the press than I found to my utter dismay that all forecasts had gone the other way. The entire picture suddenly changed. Teachers, even those tenured for years, were laid off by the thousands, never to be recalled to the classroom again.

There is a lesson to be learned from this: While you should be ever alert to trends and forecasts, it is good insurance to have a back-up skill should conditions change.

What are considered to be some of the best job opportunities in the foreseeable future?

At present, and subject to change, there is every indication that service-industry jobs will be in growing demand—jobs in sales, secretarial work, banking, accounting, and maintenance and repair of office machines and computer hardware. Advanced technology will eliminate some jobs but create others in such fields as computer engineering, software writing, and programming. The demand will grow for health-service occupations as the average life expectancy continues to increase. This will open the floodgates for employment in paramedic careers, nursing, therapy, radiology, and nuclear medicine.

In view of the fact that computerization is gradually replacing people in many of the routine office chores, what are the foreseeable career prospects for secretaries?

The prospects for secretarial positions appear excellent. In fact, they are on top of the list of demand jobs in the category of service industries.

Looking ahead, what's the likelihood that robots will start punching the clock and push human workers out of a job?

According to recent studies, it's estimated that by the end of this decade about 30% of manufacturing and industrial jobs will be taken over by sophisticated robots. It's a foregone conclusion that in time most back-breaking tasks will be handled by robots with electronic muscles and brains. This is an important fact to bear in mind in any career planning for the future. Get in a line of work where you help design and build the robots, not compete with them.

I am a student in a two-year community college, enrolled in a liberal arts program. In addition to prescribed courses for my AA degree, what skills would it be best for me to concentrate on to prepare me for gainful employment in the labor market for the foreseeable future?

For one thing, be sure to learn typing, not only for general office correspondence but for adapting it to keyboarding skills in word-processing. Other related skills you should be thinking about are those in programming and business machine maintenance, as well as the entire area of paraprofessional careers in law, medicine, and dentistry.

What are the opportunities in teaching careers?

They have never been worse. Even those who have held teaching jobs a number of years and considered the job permanent find that when the end of June comes around they are unexpectedly furloughed with no jobs to come back to in September. The lucky ones are called back if the budget allows it; the others, frustrated, leave the teaching field permanently. This situation is typical in most urban school systems.

As to salaries, professors (even those in prestigious universities) earn less than the average union electrician or truck driver.

The pendulum may swing back, but who knows when?

MISCELLANEOUS   *At 54, I have become very sensitive about my age when confronting an interviewer who is young enough to be my son. His words and action show that he's patronizing me. I can almost hear him think, "You're over the hill, Dad." What can I do to correct this impression?*

This impression may be planted in your imagination more than in fact. But be it one way or the other, when preparing for the interview, mentally go over and rehearse what you want to say about your creativity, mentioning two or three innovations you have introduced in previous firms and how profitable they turned out to be. Stress your flexibility in adapting to new conditions. Show that you have kept up with developments in your field and were personally instrumental in initiating some of them. Give specific examples to corroborate your claims.

One more thing—don't look upon the interviewer as some young Johnny-come-lately who has as yet to learn a lot. This lofty view is bound to reflect itself in your attitude. Don't assume a superior role simply because you are considerably older than he is.

I was 49 on my last birthday, but my friends tell me I don't look a day over 35. If the interviewer obtusely refers to my age, should I "post-date" it by a few years—in plain language, lie a little? I feel much younger than my chronological age.

Your friends say you don't look over 35. What say those who are not your friends? Tell the truth, but not defensively. Make it a point to emphasize how your maturity and greater experience can prove to be important assets for the job on hand.

Is there any way for a prospective employer to check on the creditation of an applicant if previous employers refuse to give out such information for fear of legal suits or bad publicity or just plain orneriness?

Yes, there is. When in doubt, an employer can require an applicant to submit to a lie detector test. Another way of checking creditation is through the National Creditation Verification Service, which has been established for that specific purpose.

I once heard a well-known corporate recruiter say that job applicants who falsify information on a resume or in an interview always stand a better chance of getting a job. Your comments?

While on the surface this seems to be an outrageous utterance to make, there is nonetheless a kernel of truth in it. An applicant can fool the interviewer (sometimes!!) and get a job through false pretenses. The consequences, however, are always risky and can lead to a pack of trouble.

A case in point is a story that made the headlines some years back. You may remember it involved a highly respected *Washington Post* reporter, a Pulitzer Prize winner who claimed among her other distinguished credentials to be a Phi Beta Kappa, and a Summa Cum Laude graduate of a prestigious university, studied at the Sorbonne, and a fluent linguist—most of which proved to be fictitious. When this was subsequently revealed to be fraudulent she was summarily fired from her job and her credibility in all other matters well-nigh destroyed.

"Oh what a tangled web we weave when first we practice to deceive!"

Does religion have any effect on work ethics?

If it did, there wouldn't be so many Gideon Bibles stolen from motel rooms every year, and there would be fewer cheaters in ethics exams in the theological seminaries.

How can you tell whether the career you have chosen is the right one for you?

As any psychologist will tell you, if you're happy in what you're doing it's the right career for you. One teacher I knew, from his first year in the classroom began to count how many more years he had to go before becoming eligible for retirement. A lawyer I chanced to meet socially confided to me that after 38 long years without personal fulfillment in the law profession, he realized that law was wrong for him. He had always liked the outdoors, he said, and had had his heart set on becoming a forester, but his father "push-guided" him into law. By contrast, I recently had occasion to chat with the pilot of a 747 jetliner and asked him, considering all the tension and responsibilities that go with the job, if he was happy in his chosen career. I shall never forget his reply: "This beats work."

What part does luck play in succeeding on the job?

Luck is good when you have it, but you can't depend on it. As one IBM executive remarked, "The harder I work, the luckier I get."

How many hours a day should I put in job hunting?

Five or six hours a day of active job hunting—library research, cold-turkey calls, interviewing—on any one day should be about the maximum. Beyond that you no longer present yourself at your very best. Leave yourself some open time for paperwork at home, as well as for social diversion with family and friends.

As a woman giving serious thoughts to entering a heretofore male-dominated occupation such as auto mechanics, what do you think the reaction of my family and friends will be?

If you have the training for the job and feel you'll be happy at it, why worry?

Unemployed at present, I am considering doing volunteer work as a public service and at the same time be usefully occupied. To what extent would volunteer work interfere with my job search?

Not seriously. In fact, it can turn out to be a decided advantage in a number of ways. From a practical point of view you have a good chance to enlarge your network of acquaintances who could possibly steer you to a job opening in your field. Then too, you have at your disposal what amounts to an answering service to take calls for you while you are away. In addition, you may have the opportunity to acquire new skills to broaden your occupational scope. To actively continue with your job search, you can always take time off for interviews whenever the occasion arises.

What measures should be considered when projecting a budget for living expenses during an extended job layoff?

Plan to cut down on non-vital expenditures such as trading in your car for a new model, taking your annual vacation, remodeling the kitchen. Eat out less frequently. Burn your credit cards—you'll be more conscious of out-of-pocket expenditures if you have to pay in hard cash.

Economize all along the line. One thing, however, you should *not* put the squeeze on—and that is the wardrobe you need for interviewing. Don't let it become seedy. If you do, you'll be hurting your chances of ever getting back on a job.

As the right-hand man of a fast-track executive known for his outstanding achievements in the financial world, how can I get his job short of committing murder?

Here is how one ingenious individual handled a situation such as yours. Unbeknownst to anyone, he forwarded a glowing dossier outlining the achievements of his superior to a leading executive recruiter who in no time at all whisked him away to a competing company at a much higher salary and a basketful of perks. Being next in line in the chain-of-command, the administrative assistant was asked to take on the vacated post.

If it worked for him, it may work for you.

It's been said many times that "push" always rates more than "pull" in any individual endeavor. What do you think?

Undeniably there is some truth in that. *Push* is necessary in the long haul, but *pull* is more immediately productive and opens the front door for you.

A story is told of a guest speaker who was invited to address a graduating class. Upon entering the auditorium he had noticed the word PUSH lettered on the door. Speaking extemporaneously to the young men and women about to join the world of work, it occurred to him to build his entire message on that one word. With that in mind, he went to great lengths to impress his audience that only through hard work and individual effort can success be achieved. To clinch his talk, he said, "Young people, in my estimation there's only one word that expresses how you can get ahead in this world—and I saw that word on the door of your auditorium as I entered." At this, all heads turned towards the door, where the word PULL stood out in bold relief.

What does "flexitime" mean?

This is an arrangement where the employee is not tied down to a definite 9-to-5 schedule and allowance is made for him to do his work according to his personal circumstances. In some cases, the employee may take work home and upon completion deliver it on a so-much-per-hour basis. Currently only a handful of the larger companies are experimenting with flexitime schedules, but the trend is growing.

Flexitime lends itself especially to such occupations as accounting, editing and indexing, textile design, commercial art, research programs, and computer software writing. In a way, flexitime is a combination of free-lance work, part-time employment, and consultative-work arrangement.

Besides marrying into the family of the Chairman of the Board, what is the surest way to get the doors open to you for a plum job?

Search out a company that's in trouble and where your special expertise would be the solution.

Is it appropriate to ask a prospective employer what his company has to offer to advance my long-range career goal?

You can do so in passing, but never lose sight of this: the employer is more concerned in what you can do for the company rather than what his company can do for you.

How long should I wait for a decision when the interviewer says, "We'll let you know."?

Don't let more than several days go by. Either write, phone, or better still, stop by personally. If you really want the job, be aggressive. Faint heart never won fair lady.

How should I proceed to let the interviewer know that upon further consideration I have decided not to accept the job?

Just as soon as you have come to that decision, contact him by phone or letter. (A letter is better.) Briefly explain the reasons why you have changed your mind. Don't fail to express appreciation for the courtesy extended to you. If you handle the situation in this manner, you don't burn the bridges behind you, should you at a later time wish to be considered for another job.

During the long interval of unemployment, I find it difficult to cope with my dwindling income. Are there professional services available to guide me in putting my finances in order?

You'll get the information you want by writing to the National Foundation for Consumer Credit, Inc., 8701 Georgia Ave., Silver Spring, MD 20910, for a directory of counseling services set up for the purpose.

I was recently laid off from a job which I believed to be permanent and in all respects right for me. I can't think of myself being out of work and have reached a point where I am willing to take on any job to overcome the rejection shock. I've been offered a position of sorts with less glittering prospects with another firm. Should I take it just to keep my thoughts away from the blitz that struck me?

Under no circumstances is it wise to take a job on the rebound. Give yourself time to become oriented to the situation. Intensify your search for a new job connection, one that is equal to or better than the job that fell apart. Never look back. Being fired from a job and latching on to another indiscriminately is not unlike marrying the first man or woman you meet in a singles bar in order to forget your recent divorce.

I have been humiliated so many times while being interviewed by a nincompoop I myself would not hire if I were an employer, that by now I've had it up to here. What's left for me to do?

Wait for Social Security (unless you've already reached that age) or visit an opthalmologist to correct your jaundiced eye. It is evident that you have been disillusioned by the entire job-search process. Unless you assume a different attitude, you'll never get a job, and if you do, you won't last long.

If offered a job out of town, how can I be sure that the job is a valid one before making moving arrangements?

Ask your would-be employer for a letter of confirmation assuring you the job is yours, naming starting date, salary and fringe benefits, who is to pay for moving expenses, etc. Go one step further. Check out the reputation of the firm by contacting the local Chamber of Commerce, the Better Business Bureau, or a related trade association.

In evaluating a company I am considering working for, how can I see what the company is really like behind the scenes if an escorted tour is not feasible?

Hint: Ask permission to visit the employee restroom. If that's poorly maintained, in disarray, in need of disinfectant, and no hand towels, you can bet dollars to doughnuts that the inner sanctum of the company is not much better in terms of work facilities and management.

This is not a question but a situation which I would like to share with others. As Administrative Assistant to the President, I proposed a plan whereby the firm could save at least $15,000 a year by cutting down coffee breaks from two 10-minute coffee breaks a day as at present, to one 15-minute break a day. Not only would this result in a sizeable savings moneywise, but it would cut down half the number of work disruptions as well. I listed other advantages. One minor point I failed to consider—how will the work force feel about it? All hell broke loose when the proposal was sprung on them, making the "Mutiny of the Bounty" seem like child's play. Result: the plan was turned down and I became the most unpopular guy in the firm and lost out on the promotion I had been expecting.

Your story reminds me about the farmer who conceived a grand idea which would positively revolutionize the egg industry, if adopted. To his way of thinking, if chickens were made to lay *rectangular* eggs rather than oval ones, there would be many advantages. Rectangular shaped eggs can be stacked easier than oval ones, they can be packed, shipped, and stored more economically, there's less breakage, etc. One thing the farmer did not take into account—how would the chickens like the idea?

Note to those on management and policy-making levels: Is there a moral somewhere in the "how would the chickens like the idea" story? Draw your own conclusions.

PERSONALITY SELF-EVALUATION QUESTIONNAIRE

In addition to inherent or acquired skills and talents, your personality has a great bearing on the type of work you are suited for as a career. To know yourself better without spending days writing up your life story, check yourself on the following as objectively as you can.

	Yes	No
Am I comparatively free of anxieties and tensions?		
Do I make friends easily?		
Am I generally well-organized?		
Do I welcome challenging assignments?		
Do I have difficulty making decisions?		
Do I like to give orders?		
Do I mind taking orders?		
Do I have the courage to speak up when I am opposed?		
Do I have the ability to convincingly present a point of view?		
Am I aware of my own biases and prejudices?		
Do I consider myself a self-starter?		
Do I have a good amount of self-confidence?		
Am I active in group affairs?		
Do I have patience for details?		
Am I a neat worker?		
Am I even-tempered?		
Am I easy to get along with?		
Do I like to work with untried ideas?		
Do I classify myself as a "takeover" person?		
Do I require drink or other stimulants to keep on going?		
Do I tend to procrastinate?		
Am I at ease speaking in public?		
Do I adjust well to a fixed schedule?		
Am I inclined to worry?		
Am I persuasive?		
Am I skillful in getting people to cooperate with me?		
Do I prefer to take the lead in a group?		
Do I have an optimistic outlook on life?		
Do people tend to like me?		
Am I a good listener?		
Do I like to work with ideas rather than with people?		
Do I have planned career goals and alternatives?		
Am I inclined to be a fatalist?		

	Yes	No
Do I learn quickly?		
Am I empathetic with the problems of others?		
Am I inclined to work better with people my own age group?		
Am I easily swayed by other people's opinions?		
Am I a persistent and steady performer?		
Do I have difficulty maintaining self-control when frustrated?		
Do I present a good image appearance-wise?		
Am I an effective negotiator?		
Do I prefer working outdoors?		
Do I resent being closely supervised?		
Am I open-minded to listen to opposing points of view?		
Do I adapt to conditions I cannot change?		
Am I innovative and creative?		
Do I pride myself in having a sense of humor?		
Do I have a retentive memory?		
Am I inclined to put career above family?		
Do I have a cooperative and understanding spouse?		
Am I efficient and dexterous?		
Do I react well to criticism and benefit by it?		
Do I smile—have a naturally happy disposition?		
Am I well-adjusted emotionally?		
Am I inclined to be enthusiastic?		
Do I have the ability to size up situations logically?		
Do I have an outgoing personality?		
Do I have good looks?		
Do I consider myself above average in intelligence?		
Am I endowed with an analytical mind?		
Do I have a wide range of interests?		
Do people often turn to me for advice?		
Am I a "soft touch?"		
Do I have the fortitude to dismiss incompetent employees?		
Do I like to read a lot?		
Am I a workaholic?		
Do I have an abiding faith in divine guidance?		

In fifty words or less:

a) How would you describe yourself?

_____

_____

_____

b) How do you think others would describe you?

_____

_____

_____

c) List your negative qualities.

_____

_____

_____

d) List your positive qualities.

_____

_____

_____

e) Describe the qualities you most admire in others that you would like to emulate.

_____

_____

_____

f) What's unique about you that is most likely to impress your interviewer?

_____

_____

_____

17

SAMPLE RESUMES

RESUME INDEX

MARY JONES
100 Main Street, PA 10000
Answering Service (100) 100-0000

* *

AVAILABLE:
Versatile, highly qualified secretary
for full-time career position as
ADMINISTRATIVE ASSISTANT

Job-related Skills:

Working knowledge of computer terminal operations (CRT)
including Cobol, Fortran, and Basic Languages; word
processing; calculator and other office machines;
typing (75 wpm); shorthand (110 wpm); technical writing
and business correspondence.

Educational Background:

Robert Morris College, Coraopolis, PA; Bachelor of
Arts, 1985. Major: Administrative Management;
Minor: Programming.
Barry Business College, Coraopolis, PA; Associate of
Arts, 1983. Major: Secretarial Science; Elective minor:
English Lit. On Dean's List for two consecutive years.

Experience:

Allegheny Temp Personnel Agency, Brentwood, PA
(1986 - Present)
Worked as Administrative Assistant on temp assignments.
Because of my diversified range of office skills and
computer knowledge, I am in high demand by local
business firms, functioning at top level immediately
without lengthy orientation.

Keystone Bros., Philadelphia, PA (1985 - 1986)
Hired as "one-girl office staff" in this newly
organized realty and architectural firm. Served as
receptionist, answered phone, arranged filing system,
did typing and shorthand, handled correspondence and
made myself generally useful. Resigned from job when
I married and moved to Brentwood, PA.

Personal:

24 years of age; 5'6", 122 lbs; excellent health.
Well groomed, of pleasing disposition, tactful.
Can shoulder responsibility without tension.

ADMINISTRATIVE ASSISTANT

TOM JONES
100 Main Street, Westport, Conn. 10000
Phone: (100) 100-0000

Mature, award-winning art director/designer/illustrator seeks affiliation with newly formed multi-media agency where he can look forward to prospect of partnership.

WORK HISTORY
(Full-time employment)

Designer/Illustrator. NBC News Center 4, New York, N.Y.
Created entire feature news format. Responsible for televised and printed graphics. Art-directed NBC's network television pilot "Coast to Coast," July 4, 1982. Co-art-directed and designed a board game aired on NBC's News Center 4 to graphically illustrate a news report on bureaucratic practices. 1978 to present.

Designer/Illustrator. ABC-TV News Graphics 7, New York, N.Y.
Director of New York graphic production. Work included designing graphics for local and network news, as well as printed jobs including the company house organ. 1973 to 1978.

Associate Animation Director. Edstan Animation Service, New York, N.Y.
Executed all stages of animated graphics, from concept to finish. Co-designer of corporate image for the television networks of CBS and WNEW Metromedia 5. 1968 to 1973.

(Freelance Employment)

Magazine layouts, logos, book design, animation, album covers. Clients include:

Art Direction Magazine	I.F. Animation Studio
Avon Books	J. Walter Thompson
Business Week Magazine	New York Magazine
CBS-TV Network	Pushpin Studio
General Foods	Random House
Harper & Row Publishers	RCA Records

ART DIRECTOR (PAGE ONE)

TOM JONES

AWARDS AND HONORS

* 1978 Emmy Award for best graphics for news program.
* Certificate of Distinction: Inclusion in the Pegasus '87 Annual of leading graphic designers.
* Composing Room Award for avant-garde book design, 1982.

EDUCATION

Pratt Institute, Brooklyn, N.Y., June 1968.
B.A. degree, major in graphic design, minor in film making.

School of Visual Art, New York, N.Y., June 1966.
A.A. degree, major in multi-media studies.

PERSONAL

Age 41; health excellent; latest medical checkup, June 1987. Single; free to relocate; former wife well-known textile designer. Finances in good order.

Tom Jones

PORTFOLIO AVAILABLE FOR REVIEW

ART DIRECTOR (PAGE TWO)

Mary Jones
100 Main Street
Austin, TX 10000
(100) 100-0000

- -

NEWLY LICENSED BEAUTICIAN

Personal Data

Age 20; 5'6", 115 lbs.; considered attractive. Often complimented for friendly disposition. Endowed with an excellent
memory for names and faces.

Education and Professional Training

Alamo Vocational High School, Austin, TX; June 1985

Exploratory courses included:

Merchandising	Interior Design
Beauty Culture	Health Care
Dress and Pattern Making	Fashion Design

*Selected Beauty Culture as two-year major.

Star School of Cosmetology; Austin, TX; June 1986.

Completed one-year professional program in cosmetology,
with emphasis on theatrical makeup, artistic hair cutting
and styling.

Related Work Experience

Neiman-Marcus, Dallas, TX; Cosmetics Department.
Sales clerk and assistant demonstrator. Summers, 1985 and 1986.

- -

If desired, will be glad to bring along model so that I may
demonstrate my artistry in makeup and hair styling.

References on hand

BEAUTICIAN

TOM JONES, CPA/MBA

100 Main Street, New York, NY 10000   (100) 100-0000

EDUCATION

1978   New York University
                   MBA, Accounting; GPA = 3.4 / 4.0

1970   Western Michigan University
                   BA, Psychology; GPA = 3.5 / 4.0

CERTIFICATION

                   Certified Public Accountant
                   State of New York

EXPERIENCE

February 1983 -   **Victor Technologies,** New York, NY
Present   NATIONAL ACCOUNTS MANAGER

                   Duties and responsibilities include:

                   - Development of direct sales of advanced 16-Bit Microcomputers to Big 8 and Big 20 CPA firms.
                   - Development and implementation of microcomputer merchandising programs including product bundling, advertising coordination and approval, trade show coordination and dealer selection/training.
                   - Evaluation of accounting and tax software for microcomputers.
                   - Closing prospective Victor dealers.
                   - Supervision of technical and marketing support personnel.

                   Accomplishments include:

                   - Successfully penetrated two (2) Big 20 accounts, one of whom will standardize on Victor products for audit purposes.
                   - Awarded the highest ratings among 31 hospitality suite vendors (91% rated very effective/effective) at the 1983 AICPA Microcomputer Conference; directed all preparation and supervised implementation.

August 1980 -   **Source Services, Inc.** New York, NY
February 1983   BRANCH MANAGER

                   A $50MM, 500 employee firm specializing in financial and data processing human resource consulting/recruiting.

                   Duties and responsibilities included:

                   - Total profit/loss responsibility for $1MM (sales) profit center.
                   - Hiring, training and supervision of professional staff of five CPA's and two CPA/MBA's and administrative staff of four.
                   - Development, review and approval of all marketing plans, client development plans and subsequent implementation.
                   - Development of all local advertising (*New York Times, CPA Journal,* etc.) and direct mail.

                   Accomplishments include:

                   - Turned around an unsuccessful New York practice, increased sales by 640% and professional staff by 350% in first full year under management.
                   - Achieved personal sales of $180K in 1981 (150% of quota), while having complete administrative responsibilities for opening two new Manhattan offices.

CERTIFIED PUBLIC ACCOUNTANT (PAGE ONE)

Source Service - accomplishments continued

- Awarded "Office of The Month" (Highest Sales per Man/Month) and "Performer of The Month" (Highest Individual Sales) in 1981.
- Brought New York branch from last in Sales per Man/Month in 1980 to first (among 15 branches) in 1981.
- Raised sales revenue from last in the company in 1980 to fourth in 1982.

June 1978 -
August 1980

ADP Network Services, New York, New York
ACCOUNT REPRESENTATIVE

A $60MM International Timesharing division of Automatic Data Processing.

Responsibilities included:

- Defining, developing and marketing financial MIS systems to major commercial banks and Fortune 500 companies.
- Successfully sold, installed and maintained the following systems: an on-line stock and bond transaction confirmation system; a data base management and graphics system for analysis of a major bank's credit card marketing efforts; a high-volume cash management system; an econometric analysis and modeling system; an on-line PERT system for management of data processing system development; varied systems used by merger and acquisition specialists to screen, analyze and generate pro-forma statements for various merger scenarios.

Accomplishments included:

- Quadrupled monthly sales in 2 years; over 100% of quota for two consecutive years.
- Closed first totally new client of econometric modeling joint venture of Townsend Greenspan Inc. and ADP.
- Developed stock confirmation system into national "product" by authoring marketing brochures, managing all organizational interfaces (DTC, ADP and banks), preparing a slide show for presentations and supervising all systems development.

May 1977 -
June 1978

Peat, Marwick, Mitchell & Co., New York, New York
ACCOUNTANT

Duties and responsibilities included:

- Evaluation of internal audit functions; evaluation of Annual Reports and 10K for compliance; review of footnotes for disclosure compliance; securities counts; evaluation of foreign affiliates equity accounting (APB-18); coordination and review of commercial bank credit files; evaluation of other accounting firms relied on by PMM; testing of transactions and schedules; evaluation of internal controls.

August 1970 -
June 1976

Agneaux Boot Co., San Francisco, California
MANAGER

Retail sales management experience as part-owner and manager of retail shoe outlet for imported footwear.

CERTIFIED PUBLIC ACCOUNTANT (PAGE TWO)

Sample Resumes

Curriculum Vitae: TOM JONES
                                               100 Main Street
                                               Princeton, NJ 10000
                                               (100) 100-0000

RESEARCH AND DEVELOPMENT PROCESS ENGINEER

EDUCATION

Undergraduate - Cooper Union, New York, NY
   Degree: B.S., 1981
   Major: Physics; Minor: Industrial Design
   Grades: 3.8 GPA/4.0

   Scholastic honors: Sigma Pi Sigma (National Physics
   Honor Society); Dean's List (every semester); First
   Prize, Cooper Union Annual Art Competition, 1978.

Graduate - Princeton University, Princeton, NJ
   Degrees: M.A., Chemical Engineering, 1983
   Ph.D., Chemical Engineering (expected June 1987).

   Scholastic honors: TRI Research Fellowship; Sigma Xi.

   Campus activities: Social Events Chairman, Princeton
   University Graduate School (600 students); intramural
   soccer and volleyball; founder of microphotography club.

WORK EXPERIENCE

1983 - 1986
   Teaching Assistant, Department of Chemical Engineering,
   Princeton University. Heat, Mass, and Momentum Transfer
   (undergraduate course). Mathematical Analysis for Engineers (graduate course).

1981 - 1983
   Laboratory Assistant, Physics Department, Cooper Union.
   Designed new experiments for sophomore physics laboratory.
   Tutored students in physics and mathematics.

CHEMICAL ENGINEER (PAGE ONE)

PAPERS PRESENTED AND PUBLISHED

- "Utilization of Wetting Force Measurements for the Physical and Chemical Characterization of Fiber Surfaces," in collaboration with Bernard Miller, presented at the Colloquium of the Physics and Fiber Surfaces, TRI, Princeton, NJ, May 3, 1987; to be published in a future issue of <u>Textile Research Journal</u>.

- "Extended Analysis and Application of Wetting Force Measurements," in collaboration with Bernard Miller, presented at the Fiber society 1985 Technical Conference, Charlottesville, VA.

- "Influence of the Braid on Transition Temperatures as Obtained by Torsional Braid Analyses," submitted to Polymer Engineering and Science, 1986.

PERSONAL INFORMATION

- Date of birth: December 2, 1959; naturalized U.S. citizen.
- Foreign languages: Persian, Arabic, and Hebrew.
- Avocation: Metal sculpture. My work was selected for exhibition in commercial galleries. Money earned from sales covered most of my educational expenses.

CHEMICAL ENGINEER (PAGE TWO)

TOM JONES
100 Main Street
New York, NY 10000
(100) 100-0000

COMMUNICATIONS MEDIA SPECIALIST

SCHOLASTIC BACKGROUND

University of Pittsburgh, Pittsburgh, PA
Bachelor of Arts, May 1977; Summa Cum Laude
Major: Communications; Minor: Marketing and Merchandising

High School of Art and Design, New York, NY
Graduated: June 1973; class valedictorian
Awarded four-year scholarship to University of Pittsburgh

EMPLOYMENT BACKGROUND

Media Buyer
Gulf Advertising, New York, NY. October 1982 to present.
Started as Media Assistant and shortly after was promoted to position
of Media Buyer (radio, TV, and print), with broader responsibilities
and substantial increase in salary.

Market Manager
Ace Promotions, Inc., New York, NY. May 1980 to October 1982.
Initiated and coordinated all aspects of promotion to publicize new line of
Hershey products, involving special events, sports complexes and stadiums
for sampling. Recruited, trained, and managed local models as sampling
personnel. Arranged for TV and newspaper coverage.

Assistant Manager
Renegade Clothing Store, Scarsdale, NY. March 1978 to May 1980.
Monitored sales and inventory; coordinated all interior and window dis-
plays for the store; served as liaison with the ad agency.

Assistant Promotion Director
Fashion Institute of Technology, New York, NY. July 1977 to March 1978.
Responsible for layout, writing, and editing of monthly newsletter and press
releases for the F.I.T. Alumni Association.

➡

COMMUNICATIONS MEDIA SPECIALIST (PAGE ONE)

TOM JONES   Page 2

INTERNSHIPS (1976-1977)

<u>General Assistant and Gofer</u>
Creative Events, Inc., Pittsburgh, PA
Involved with the creation, distribution, and promotional campaigns
for retail outlets.

<u>Assistant to Public Relations Director</u>
Performing Arts for Community Education, Pittsburgh, PA
Helped prepare and send out press releases for coming events.

<u>Assistant to Associate Producer</u>
"Saturday Magazine On-the-Air for Young Executives" radio program,
Station WRTZ, Pittsburgh, PA.
Involved with contacting personalities for interviews.

PERSONAL

Born May 2, 1955, height 5'10", weight 162 lbs.
Tiptop physical condition, nonsmoker.
Happily married, two great kids.
Active in civic and community organizations.
Outgoing personality, makes friends easily.

Tom Jones

Verifiable credentials available

COMMUNICATIONS MEDIA SPECIALIST (PAGE TWO)

TOM JONES
100 Main Street, Waltham, Mass. 10000 Phone: (100) 100-0000

■

┌─────── COMPUTER ELECTRONICS TECHNICIAN ───────┐
│ seeks entry-level position where utilization of │
│ training may be best applied to a growth- │
│ oriented company in the computer field. │
└───┘

EDUCATION:

> <u>Boston College</u>, Chestnut Hill, Mass. B.S. degree,
> June 1986. Major in Physics; Minor in English
> Literature.
>
> <u>GTE Sylvania Technical School</u>, Waltham, Mass.
> Graduate, Computer Electronics Course, June 1987. Studies
> included microprocessor techniques and 8086 timing and
> operation; minicomputer operation and maintenance with
> troubleshooting at the component level; interfacing
> techniques in both hardware and software areas. Also
> basic electricity, electronics, and digital fundamentals.

RELATED WORK EXPERIENCE: *(part-time and summers, '84 to '87)*

> <u>Lawrence Electronic Distributors, Inc.</u>, Boston, Mass.
> Helped prepare news releases and other promotional
> writing. Represented the company in a number of
> electronic shows and exhibitions that demonstrated the
> superiority of high-tech products produced by the company.
> Was offered a full-time position as Assistant Public
> Relations Director, but decided against it to be able to
> continue with my education.

> <u>Bradford Resource Center</u>, Cambridge, Mass.
> Responsibilities included servicing investments in the BRC
> Fund, an assignment that involved a substantial amount of
> computer interaction and a comprehension of peripheral
> terminology.

PERSONAL:

> Age 23; height 5'11"; weight 170 lbs.; single; no
> encumbrances. Travel or relocation poses no problem.

> *Please note: Opportunity to advance
> is more important than starting
> salary.*

COMPUTER ELECTRONICS TECHNICIAN

MARY JONES
100 Main Street
Brighton, MA 100000
(100) 100-0000

A challenging position as
COMPUTER TRAINING SPECIALIST
preferably in metropolitan New York area

EXPERIENCE

Professional Software, Inc., Needham, MA.   8/84 – Present
Manufacturers and distributors of software for IBM, Texas
Instruments, Compaq, and Digital microcomputers.

Dealer Training/Support Representative
Self-designed position involving conducting Product/Sales
Training Program for nationwide dealer base and corporate
accounts; creating training manuals, visual aids and dealer
training materials; developing and implementing policies and
procedures for the IBM Support Department; devising systems of
communication between all internal departments regarding
product development.

Dealer Sales/Support Representative
Telemarketing and dealer support position involving establishment of new product in highly competitive marketplace;
development of 200 dealerships in midwestern U.S. and western
Canada; coordination of departmental reports, forms, logs;
competition research.

New England Electronics, Needham, MA.   7/82 – 8/84

Assistant Manager
Administrative/support work for microcomputer system sales
department. Helped write instructional manuals.

Brett Junior High School, Tamworth, NH.   9/81 – 6/82

Licensed Language Arts Teacher
Taught grades 6,7,8 in areas of reading comprehension,
spelling, and grammar. Assisted in designing and developing
writing program which, upon evaluation, was approved and
incorporated in the curriculum.

EDUCATION

Springfield College, Springfield, MA. Bachelor of Science in
Elementary Education with concentrations in English,
Psychology, and Reading. Graduated top of the class, 5/81.

In addition to my formal education, completed several workshop
courses in computer programming and sales strategies.

INTERESTS

Photography, physical fitness, painting.

COMPUTER TRAINING SPECIALIST

MARY JONES, 100 Main Street, Chicago, IL 10000
Business Phone: (100) 100-0000 Home Phone: (100) 100-0000

CUSTOMER SERVICE MANAGER

● **EXPERIENCE:**

1983-Present

Customer Service Representative
Budget Rent-a-Car, Chicago, IL
Maintain personal contact in a fast-paced
environment with clients' needs and preferences.
Basic responsibilities include phone reservations, input of daily receipts, cash rentals,
and computerized check-ins. Currently assist
marketing and promotion department by setting up
eye-catching promotional material for distribution to prospective clients and travel agents.
Help plan and coordinate trade shows.

1981-1983
(after school
hours and
weekends)

Hostess-Waitress
Purple Lounge, Chicago, IL
Responsibilities included greeting and seating
customers, serving cocktails and dinners. At
times, assisted with planning menus and customer
special requests. Frequently complimented by
customers for personal attention shown them.
Received special citation and bonus by owner for
meritorious service.

● **EDUCATION:**

North Chicago Community College, Chicago, IL
A.A. degree, Business Management, June 1983.
Career related courses: Human Relations, Econo-
mics, Statistics, Speech, and Fundamentals of
Travel Industry encompassing ticketing tour
promotions, hotel/motel and car rentals, air-
line reservations.
Completed Dale Carnegie course in Human
Relations and Selling.

● **PERSONAL:**

Born: May 15, 1963; exuberant health; 5'6",
120 lbs.
Athletically inclined - swimming, jogging,
biking. Happy disposition, outgoing personality, tactful.

CUSTOMER SERVICE MANAGER

TOM JONES
100 Main Street, Salt Lake City, Utah 10000 Phone: (100) 100-0000

FINANCIAL SERVICES PROFESSIONAL
Investment Planning/Pension Funds/Municipal Securities/Insurance

AREAS OF EXPERTISE

licences and certifications	Certified in Series 7, Series 52MSRB, Series 63 and Series 24. Fully licensed in State of Utah to sell life, health, variable annuities and disability insurance.
business start up	Opened own brokerage business with limited capital, and within a short time developed it to service more than 100 accounts in a broadening field of operations.
management and sales	Proven know-how in selling bonds, securities, insurance, real estate, implementing venture capital projects, managing estates.

BUSINESS EXPERIENCE

MANAGING PARTNER 1984-Present	Jones-Allan, Inc., Salt Lake City, Utah Founded the company, drawing together 30 prime shareholders and as a working member of the Board of Directors, serve as Secretary/Treasurer. One of a three-person management team, supervise operations on a day-to-day basis, with responsibilities in managing pension funds, budgeting, forward planning and personnel recruitment. Work on a daily basis with investors of yearly incomes of $75,000 to $2-million, and with corporations earning from $100,000 to $20-million.
SECURITIES REP 1982-1984	Stanford Horst, Inc., Salt Lake City, Utah Started as a trainee and within a two-year period was successful in opening over 100 new accounts. Sold municipal bonds and fixed securities, such as corporate, GNMA's, treasuries. Promoted to Assistant Vice President.

FINANCIAL SERVICES PROFESSIONAL (PAGE ONE)

LOAN OFFICER   <u>Union Savings and Loan, Salt Lake City, Utah</u>
1980-1982   Was hired as Teller and advanced to position of Loan Officer within six months. Selected twice as "Employee of the Month." Received substantial increase in salary.

EDUCATION

1978-1980   <u>M.A. - Syracuse University, Syracuse, New York</u>
Maxwell School of Citizenship and Public Affairs. Majored in Political Science.

1974-1978   <u>B.A. - Syracuse University, Syracuse, New York</u>
Majored in Business Administration and Finance.

PERSONAL

Born May, 1956. Married; 2 children; wife, history teacher in local high school.

Finances in good order; drive late model car.

Fluent in French and German; some Spanish.

Both my wife and I are active in various civic and charitable organizations - United Way, American Red Cross, Community Better Citizenship League.

Past earnings over $100,000 annually.

FINANCIAL SERVICES PROFESSIONAL (PAGE TWO)

TOM JONES
100 Main Street, St. Petersburg, FL 10000
Phone: (100) 100-0000

OBJECTIVE: To obtain a challenging position in the field
                   of health education in a community or
                   industrial environment.

EDUCATION: Florida State University, Tallahassee, FL.
                   B.S. degree in Health Education, June 1986.

                   St. Petersburg Junior College, FL.
                   A.A. degree in Biology, June 1984.

PROFESSIONAL   Bayfront Medical Center, St. Petersburg, FL.
EXPERIENCE: Six-month internship with the Employee Well-
                   ness Program. Participated in citywide health
                   screening. Helped prepare a number of infor-
                   mative brochures on the problems of hyperten-
                   sive individuals in the workforce.
                   January to June 1986.

                   Governor's Health Fair, Tallahassee, FL.
                   Recruited and coordinated fifty volunteers
                   for this important event. The Fair was an
                   unprecedented success, and I was among those
                   given credit for helping to make it so.
                   August 1986.

                   Leon County School System, Tallahassee, FL.
                   Was instrumental in organizing an educational
                   program for teenage mothers still attending
                   school, covering such matters as infant care,
                   nutrition, and professional resources.
                   September to December 1985.

VOLUNTEER   o Active in "Eye Care" sight preservation
WORK: program.
                   o Frequently lecture in neighborhood schools
                     on the dangers of drug abuse.
                   o Auxiliary driver, senior citizen health
                     service bus.

HEALTH EDUCATION SPECIALIST

MARY JONES
100 Main Street
Boston, Mass. 10000
Phone: (100) 100-0000

JOB OBJECTIVE

Entry-level position in the field of
HUMAN RESOURCES MANAGEMENT/PERSONNEL ADMINISTRATION

PROFILE

- Career-oriented college graduate with B.S. degree
in Behavioral Science; excellent communication and
interpersonal skills and total commitment to succeed
in chosen field. Worked throughout school years
(part-time and summers) to help finance educational
costs, while at the same time gaining hands-on
experience in customer relations, working harmoniously
with people of all ages, backgrounds, and temperaments.

- Trained in personnel administration, industrial
psychology, stress management, economics, statistics,
and other studies relevant to career goal. Knowledge
of basic computerized operations.

- Plans to pursue postgraduate studies (evenings)
towards an M.A. in Human Resources Management.

EDUCATION

B.S., Boston University, Boston, Mass., June 1986.
Majored in Behavioral Science, minored in Social
Studies; graduated top 10 percentile of class.

Extracurricular activities: President of senior class.
Organized student committee for urban problems, with
special emphasis on child abuse and the destitute
elderly in the greater Boston area.

HUMAN RESOURCES MANAGER (PAGE ONE)

MARY JONES   Page 2

EMPLOYMENT HISTORY

1986 to present: Assistant Manager, Olympiad Lounge, Boston, Mass. Principal activities center on interfacing with kitchen personnel and serving staff; helping to maintain high standards in quality control and customer satisfaction, assist in the hiring, training, and supervision of staff.

7/85 to 9/85 (summer) Hostess, Bennigan's Restaurant, Boston, Mass. Responsibilities included greeting guests, assigning tables, scheduling waitresses, and generally ensuring adherence to established company policies and practices.

5/84 to 8/84 (summer) Hostess Trainee, Steak and Ale, Boston, Mass. Carried out responsibilities similar to those described above.

Prior experience: Employed during high school vacations as cashier and sales clerk, Cunningham Drugs, Boston, Mass. Operated computerized cash register and helped with inventory.

PERSONAL

Born in Paris, France, March 1964. Attractive, well groomed, endowed with good health and excellent memory. Fluent in French and Spanish. Height, 5'5"; weight, 115 lbs; single, unencumbered. Self-starter, a good listener, and active doer.

Travel or relocation presents no problem.

HUMAN RESOURCES MANAGER (PAGE TWO)

TOM JONES

100 Main Street, Chicago, IL 10000   Phone (100) 100-0000

Marketing Management Specialist

My 14 years of experience encompasses all phases of marketing and marketing management. Beginning with product development for a major retailer and catalog operation, I have moved through a series of increasingly responsible positions with companies such as General Electric and Sperry Remington, and in my latest assignment am Product Development Manager for Wang, Inc. Throughout my career, I have shown a consistent talent for spotting trends in consumer preferences and for reaching these markets through the creation of new products or redirection of marketing efforts.

Selected Career Highlights

In 1980 I was recruited by Wang, Inc. as one of its **Product Development Managers**. In this role, I direct interdivisional marketing programs, working with senior management from the divisions on the coordination of worldwide marketing efforts. These include the development of new business through major credit card companies such as American Express, Visa, Carte Blanche and others, collaborating with hotels and airlines on the creation of joint marketing ventures and devising direct mail programs.

During this time I have:

o <u>Gained the highest response rates in the industry for a test market program</u>. Indications are that a worldwide launch of the program and creation of a marketing communications vehicle could cut current duplicate efforts, eliminate direct billing receivables, and produce savings of up to $2 million annually.

o <u>Managed a program for a top-rank marketing segment</u>. Developed an effective sales tool and a series of products which made inroads into a new market which should build product loyalty, increase sales, and open up this market to additional services.

MARKETING MANAGEMENT SPECIALIST (PAGE ONE)

TOM JONES

Page Two

o <u>Created advertising and promotional programs</u>, specializing in print advertising, for major publications, as part of cooperative product development efforts with other large corporations.

o <u>Conducted worldwide market research</u> for possible new product categories, many of them joint development efforts with major companies, including national and international financial institutions.

Earlier Experience

Sperry Remington. . . . . **Product Manager**
Provided a link between sales and marketing for a $25 million product line. Conducted competitive analyses by product area; wrote business plans and promotional programs; advised on packaging; enhanced brand awareness; advised on sales training. Identified a new market as a profitable business venture to augment existing product lines. This allowed for common usage of manufacturing facilities, distribution channels, and market strategies. Executive of America Award for outstanding achievement.

General Electric. . . . . **Home Economist-Product Development**
Formulated new product concepts based on consumer preferences. Managed new product introduction and presented these products to the national sales force. Appraised competitive position of our products; participated in strategic planning; coordinated and supervised all photo "shoots" involving these products, wrote all consumer-directed copy and reviewed packaging and promotional copy.

Montgomery Ward . . . . **Corporate Home Economist**
This was an entry-level position encompassing broad-based market research and promotional activity. It included product testing, public relations, radio and television presentations, and liaison with R&D professionals.

Education

M.B.A., Marketing Research, University of Illinois.
B.A., Communications, Ohio State University.

References

Please defer contacting previous employers until a hiring determination is given serious consideration.

MARKETING MANAGEMENT SPECIALIST (PAGE TWO)

MARY JONES
100 Main Street, New York, NY 10000
(100) 100-0000

CAREER OBJECTIVE: Desire trainee position as assistant curator in
                   art museum or private gallery, hoping eventually to rise
                   to the rank of head curator. Am planning to relocate to
                   my home town in Houston, Texas.

EDUCATION: Graduate, High School of Music and Art, New York, NY, 1981.
            Awarded four-year scholarship to NYU, earning BA degree in
            Fine Arts - 1985.
            Attended evening program at the Art Students League, New
            York, studying under Hans Hoffman, Al Hollingsworth, and
            Chaim Gross.

RECORD OF EXHIBITIONS *(Solo and Group Shows)*:
            o Ward-Nasse Gallery, New York, NY.
            o Lehman College Art Gallery, Bronx, NY.
            o Trinity Gallery of Modern Art, San Francisco, CA.
            o Yodfat Fine Art Gallery, Tel Aviv, Israel.

PROFESSIONAL EXPERIENCE: On staff of exhibit and display department,
            Yeshiva University, New York, NY, working under Sylvia
            Axelrod, department head. Duties include arranging and
            mounting exhibit material, attending to correspondence,
            proofreading museum bulletins, making myself generally
            useful. June 1985-present.

PERSONAL INFORMATION: Age 23; 5'5"; 115 lbs.; single.
            o Linguistically inclined; speak and write Hebrew, French,
              and German.
            o Favorite hobbies and activities: In addition to jogging,
              bike riding, and morning workouts, indulge in reading
              books on history of art (ancient and modern), photography,
              printmaking.
            o Outstanding characteristics: Commended for organizational
              ability and great team work, ready to pitch in beyond the
              regular work day to meet deadline schedules and openings.

MUSEUM CURATOR

MARY JONES
100 Main Street
West Palm Beach, FL 10000
Phone: (100) 100-0000

* * * * * * * *

OBJECTIVE:
To make effective use of my professional experience,
educational background, and personal attributes
in a supervisory position in the nursing field.

EDUCATION:
Florida International University, North Miami, FL
B.S.N. in Nursing, graduated April 1985. Inducted
into FIU Nursing Honor Society, 1985.

Florida State University, Tallahassee, FL
B.S. in Liberal Arts, graduated June 1980. Majored
in Psychology with a minor in Recreational Therapy.
Maintained a 3.3. G.P.A.

LICENSURE:
Florida State Board of Nursing, September 1985.
#1644082.

EXPERIENCE:
1985 to present
NICU Staff Nurse, Jackson Memorial Hospital, Miami, FL

Duties include physical assessment of neonatal infants,
administering prescribed medications and treatments,
working with emergency medical unit, writing up case
histories. Recommended by hospital administrator for
Special Merit Award.

1981 to 1983
Recreational Therapist, Hillsborough Hospital, Tampa, FL

Duties included development, planning, implementation,
and supervision of leisure skill activities for psychi-
atric patients in a wide range of age categories. Co-
therapist for Skills Enhancement Training Program. Actively participated in multi-departmental staff meetings.

NURSING SUPERVISOR (PAGE ONE)

MARY JONES   Page 2

1980 to 1981
<u>Assistant Program Coordinator</u>, Center for Continuing
Education, University of South Florida, Tampa, FL

Duties included general assistance to program coordinator. Participated in interviews with new members
of the instructional staff and assigning classrooms.
Helped with student registration and programming. Cred-
ited with devising a system which was instrumental in
alleviating scheduling difficulties.

<u>ABOUT MYSELF</u>:
- Height: 5'3"; weight 110 lbs.; health excellent;
  single.
- Naturalized American citizen, born in Cuba, May 1960.
- Athletically inclined, with special interest in tennis
  and swimming. Have instructed small groups in aerobic
  dancing.
- Have done volunteer hospital work while still a
  student in high school.
- Personal attributes: good disposition, always compas-
  sionate but never maudlin. Get along well with medical staff and co-workers.

        Letters of commendation from schools
        and employers available on request.

NURSING SUPERVISOR (PAGE TWO)

MARY JONES   100 Main Street
                                    Atlanta, GA 10000
                                    (100) 100-0000

OBJECTIVE: Executive-level position as Office
                  Manager with large corporation.

NATURE OF   Over fifteen years of practical exper-
EXPERIENCE: ience in diversified secretarial work
                  with growing administrative duties that
                  involve overall smooth flow of office
                  operations and supervision of staff.

                  Working knowledge of:
                   Word processing   Data processing
                   Typing (75 wpm)   Desktop publishing
                   Steno (120 wpm)   Bookkeeping
                   Copy-editing   Telecommunications

EMPLOYMENT   B'nai B'rith Youth Organization,
HISTORY: Atlanta, GA, September 1980 - Present
                  SECRETARY/BOOKKEEPER
                     Responsible for general office
                  management; preparing monthly financial
                  reports; general bookkeeping including
                  a/p, a/r; editing BBYO newsletter;
                  correspondence; purchasing of office
                  equipment and supplies; liaison with
                  parents and youth counselors.

                  Atlas Paint Company, Atlanta, GA
                  June 1975 - July 1980
                  PART OWNER
                     After five years as homemaker and
                  mother of two, returned to the business
                  world as part-owner of this company.
                     Specifically responsible for payroll,
                  customer service, purchasing supplies
                  and equipment, billing, recruiting and
                  hiring of help. In this enterprise I

OFFICE MANAGER (PAGE ONE)

EMPLOYMENT   was successful in establishing highly
HISTORY   profitable business contacts with
(continued)   private and commercial realtors. Upon
                   developing an allergic reaction to
                   oil-base paints and solvents, it was
                   necessary for me to terminate my
                   connections with the firm--which I did
                   on a most amicable basis.

                   American Fruit Shippers, Atlanta, GA
                   January 1968 - January 1970
                   <u>HEAD BOOKKEEPER</u>
                      In the first three months on the job,
                   I introduced an automated bookkeeping
                   system, using the latest available
                   equipment. With a minimum office staff,
                   kept all financial records for this firm
                   with an annual cash flow of over
                   $500,000. Saved over $4,000 yearly on
                   cash discounts which in the past were
                   neglected, plus additional income tax
                   deductions. Left to get married and
                   raise a family.

EDUCATION: University of Georgia, Atlanta, GA
                   B.A. in Business Administration
                   June 1968

                   Keene Business College, Keene, NJ
                   A.A. in Secretarial Studies
                   June 1966

ABOUT   Born: April 6, 1946
MYSELF   Height: 5'4"; weight: 112 lbs.
                   Married to C.P.A.; two teenage children.
                   People-oriented, self-motivated, tactful.
                   Enjoy gourmet cooking, interior decorating,
                   sewing and needlework, theater, jogging.

                              Available for interviews
                              and review of credentials
                              at any time.

OFFICE MANAGER (PAGE TWO)

TOM JONES
100 Main Street
Riviera Beach, FL 10000
Phone: (100) 100-0000

PROJECT MANAGER OR ON-SITE SUPERINTENDENT
IN THE SOUTH FLORIDA CONSTRUCTION INDUSTRY

PROFILE: <u>Background includes</u>: Residential and commercial
            building contracting, additions, alterations as well
            as remodeling. Familiar with all related trades and
            materials.

            <u>Experience includes</u>: Project management; layouts;
            construction take-offs; estimating; quality control;
            blueprint reading; carpentry.

WORK   <u>Full-charge Production Manager</u> ....1979 - Present
HISTORY: Remodeling Contractors Inc., Mamaroneck, NY.

            Well-known specialists in private home
            alterations. It is my responsibility to hire and
            supervise work crews in various categories and
            trades. Work closely with estimating department,
            engineers and suppliers. Greatly due to my own
            efforts, construction costs invariably are well
            within budget figures. The frequent bonuses I
            receive are indicative of my value to the
            company.

            <u>Owner-operator</u> ....1969 - 1979
            American All-Crafts Company, Irvington, NY.

            This home improvements company which I started
            on a small scale grew into a very lucrative
            enterprise due to superior craftsmanship and
            attention to detail, with net income increasing
            30% annually. The company was bought out by
            Remodeling Contractors Inc., where I was
            subsequently hired as Full-charge Production
            Manager on a generous salary and commission
            basis.

PROJECT MANAGER (PAGE ONE)

<u>Master Carpenter</u> ....1963 - 1969
Amato Construction Company, Tarrytown, NY.

Supervised 10-man crew. This position called for
thorough familiarity with estimating, carpentry and
allied crafts, building code requirements and safety
regulations.

<u>Carpenter and Cabinet Maker</u> ....1960 - 1963
AAA Cabinet and General Carpentry, Yonkers, NY.

First exposure to the professional carpentry field.
After a short apprenticeship was promoted to the
position of full-fledged carpenter.

EDUCATION: A.A., Construction and Mechanical Technology, 1960
              Westchester Community College, Westchester, NY.

              General Diploma, major in Woodshop & Drafting, 1958
              Brooklyn Technical High School, Brooklyn, NY.

              Extracurricular activities in both schools included
              stage set design and construction for school plays.

PERSONAL: Born June 18, 1941; height 6'2"; weight 190 lbs.
              Excellent health: latest medical checkup, May 1987.
              Perfect vision: 20/20 without glasses.
              Married; two sons in U.S. Air Force.

              Member, Association of Home Industrial Builders,
                      Construction Consultants Group of America.

                                          REFERENCES ON HAND

PROJECT MANAGER (PAGE TWO)

TOM JONES

100 Main Street, New York, NY 10000   (100) 100-0000

PERSONAL PROFILE   Flexible, self-motivated sales professional with entrepreneurial instincts, experienced in microcomputer sales. Consistent record of first-rank sales growth and excellent client relations.

Strengths: Drive, coupled with organizational skills and the ability to motivate others. An analytical ability to penetrate to the heart of problems and propose solutions.

PROFESSIONAL EXPERIENCE

1982 to Present   **Corporate Sales Representative,** Computerland—Wall Street, NY, NY
National Accounts Sales Representative of Corporate Sales Division. Developed accounts by establishing relationships with corporate purchasing agents and data processing professionals of Fortune 50, 100 and 500 companies. Responsible for negotiating volume purchase agreements for hardware, software, maintenance and training; servicing and supporting users.

Key Accomplishments: Landed the largest single account with yearly sales of $1.2 million. Have been the top performer in New York since January 1983; averaging $250K monthly sales. Achieved distinction of Sales Representative for the month of September in Computerland network: 500 stores, 2,000 reps.

1981 to 1982   **Self-Employed,** San Francisco and New York
Small business computer and word processing consultant. Automated manual budget and expense procedures for tracking and analysis. Defined databases for report generation. Conducted in-house client training.

EDUCATION

1977-1981   B.A., St. John's College, Annapolis, Maryland
The St. John's program is a four-year, structured curriculum that concentrates on exploring the basic skills of analytic and synthetic thinking by examining the systems developed by the great thinkers of the Western World in an interactive environment.

MILITARY SERVICE

1973 to 1976   Presidential Security and Ceremonial Battalion
Marine Barracks, 8th & I Streets, S.E., Washington, D.C.
Personnel Administration. Conducted interviews for new personnel background investigations to determine security status for assignment to the White House and Camp David.

Current Status   No obligation.   Discharge: Honorable.   Rank: Corporal.

SALES REPRESENTATIVE

TOM JONES

100 Main Street, Monticello, N.Y. 10000 Phone: (100) 100-0000

SCHOOL PSYCHOLOGIST

Education
M.A. degree in Psychology - emphasis on pre-teens.
State University of New York, Monticello, N.Y. June 1986.

B.S. degree in Human Development and Family Relations.
State University of New York, Monticello, N.Y. June 1984.
   Graduated top ten percentile of class.
   Elected to Kappa Delta Pi Honor Society.

Licensure
Granted New York State license as School Psychologist,
September 1986.

Internship
Sullivan County School System, N.Y.
Fall 1985 to Spring 1986.
   Work consisted of counseling and testing; meeting with
   groups as well as individual students on a one-to-one
   basis; consulting with parents, teachers, and referral
   agencies; writing up case histories of youngsters showing tendencies towards various kinds of exceptionality.

Skills
- Proficiency in administering and interpreting aptitude,
  achievement, and personality tests.
- Concise and clear communication in documenting verbal
  and written reports.
- Analyzing emotional characteristics which have a direct
  or peripheral bearing on social behavior, often resulting in learning difficulties.
- Ability to win the trust and confidence of children known
  to be non-communicative.

Personal
Helped finance college education working part-time as
reading tutor, camp counselor, and teacher aide.
Active in charitable and civic organizations.
Member, National Association of School Psychologists.

SCHOOL PSYCHOLOGIST

TOM JONES
100 Main Street
New York, NY 10000
(100) 100-0000

* *

SCREEN PRINTING TECHNOLOGIST
Now semi-retired, offers his professional services
to the trade as a freelance consultant.

PROFESSIONAL BACKGROUND

1965 - 1985   <u>Art Director/Production Manager</u>, Atlas Printing and Display Co., Inc., New York, NY.
Under my supervision, this company grew to become one of the nation's leading specialists in screen printing reproduction of posters, displays, and point-of-purchase advertising.

1957 - 1965   <u>Assistant Professor</u>, Graphic Arts Department, College of Design and Printing, Brooklyn, NY.
Organized and supervised screen printing classes; developed courses of study, ordered supplies and equipment; recruited teaching staff from the trade, orienting them to classroom teaching procedures.

PUBLISHED WORKS

Author of a number of books on screen printing and the graphic arts. *Screen Printing as a Fine and Commercial Art*, published by McGraw-Hill Book Co., is generally considered to be the basic reference manual on the craft.

Articles on screen printing technology regularly appear in such trade and professional journals as:
Signs of the Times, Graphic Arts Monthly, American Artist, Printing News, Screen Printing.

SCREEN PRINTING TECHNOLOGIST (PAGE ONE)

* *

EDUCATIONAL BACKGROUND

1949 - 1951   <u>Rhode Island School of Design</u>, Providence, RI.
                M.A. degree in Printing Technology.

1945 - 1949   <u>Columbia University</u>, New York, NY.
                B.S. degree in Graphic Design.

ARMY SERVICE

1951 - 1957   Lieutenant, Quartermasters, U.S. Army,
                Aberdeen, MD.
                In charge of purchasing printing equipment and related
                supplies. Awarded special citation for keeping well
                within budget. Subsequently promoted to the rank of
                Captain.

PERSONAL

                60 years young; 6'3", 195 lbs.;
                in excellent health.
                Most recent medical checkup, March 1987.
                Willing to travel wherever my services are required.

ADDITIONAL INFORMATION

                Honorary Life Member, Advisory Commission;
                High School of Art & Design, New York, NY.

                Honored by the SPPA for outstanding contributions to
                the screen printing industry.

                Listed in *Who's Who in American Graphic Arts*.
                Frequently called in as expert in court litigations in-
                volving the screen printing process.

SCREEN PRINTING TECHNOLOGIST (PAGE TWO)

TOM JONES
100 Main Street
Detroit, Michigan 10000
(100) 100-000

CAREER
OBJECTIVE:
To be professionally affiliated with private or government agency involved in urban development and related social issues.

EDUCATION:
B.S. degree, Summa Cum Laude, University of Michigan, June 1987.
Major in urban studies, minor in sociology and statistics.

Courses in line with career objective include:

History of Urban System	Sociology
Statistical Surveys	Computer Programming Basics
The Legislative Process	Urban Economics
Transportation Planning	Metropolitan Problems

INTRA-SCHOOL
ACTIVITIES:
Captain, University of Michigan Squash Team for two consecutive years.

One of six students chosen to represent my home town, Detroit, in its annual student exchange program with Toyota City, Japan, Summer of 1984.

RELATED
WORK
EXPERIENCE:

(summers and school vacations)

Intern for State Congressman of my district. Basically, my work consisted in preparing synopses of congressional proceedings for his study and review; proofreading newsletters to constituents; helping with general correspondence in addition to taking care of the usual office routines. Letter of high commendation attests to my performance.

SOCIOLOGIST (PAGE ONE)

Statistical Survey Taker for feasibility research group, Ann Arbor, Michigan. In this capacity, conducted countywide telephone survey regarding transportation needs in Washtenaw. Also assisted in compilation of data gathered.

General Helper for Kean's Detroit Yacht Harbor, Detroit, Michigan. Worked on gas docks and, on occasion, clerked in the marina hardware supply store.

OFFICE
SKILLS: Typing - 70 wpm; steno - 105 wpm.
Working knowledge of word processing and basic programming.

PERSONAL: Age 22; height 5'11"; weight 162 lbs.
health excellent, latest medical checkup, June 1987.

Fluent in Spanish, some French.
Athletically inclined. In addition to squash, my favorite sports activities are swimming, surfing, and jogging.

REFERENCES: Verifiable records available for your review.

Tom Jones

SOCIOLOGIST (PAGE TWO)

MARY JONES
100 Main Street
Richmond, VA 10000
Phone: (100) 100-0000

Fully matriculated Speech and Hearing Therapist seeks private or government position in her chosen career.

EDUCATION

University of North Carolina, Chapel Hill, NC.
Master of Science in Speech Pathology, 1986.

University of Maryland, College Park, MD.
Bachelor of Arts in Hearing and Speech Sciences, 1984.

CLINICAL EXPERIENCE
(1984 - 1986)

North Carolina Memorial Hospital Hearing and Speech Clinic, Chapel Hill, NC.

Diagnosis of speech/language disorders and subsequent rehabilitation for the neurologically impaired. Alaryngeal speech therapy, fluency therapy, articulation therapy, and hearing screenings.

University of North Carolina, Division of Speech and Hearing, Chapel Hill, NC.

Voice and articulation therapy. Development of a home program for young children; stuttering evaluations and therapy for individuals of various ages.

Duke University, Developmental Evaluation Center, Durham, NC.

Diagnosis of language and learning disorders of children. Heavy emphasis on accurate report writing of patient's medical file.

SPEECH AND HEARING THERAPIST (PAGE ONE)

MARY JONES   Page 2

University of North Carolina, Hearing Impaired Pre-school, Chapel Hill, NC.

Group and individual speech/language therapy, simulating a classroom setting for children with hearing difficulties.

EXTRACURRICULAR VOLUNTEER WORK

University of North Carolina, Division for Disorders of Development and Learning, Chapel Hill, NC.

Participated in experimental stimulation program for young children nine weeks to thirty-six months. (March 1985 - May 1985)

Kendall Demonstration Elementary School, Division of Gallaudet College for the Deaf, Washington, DC.

Assisted with individual speech therapy for deaf children and teaching survival skills to a group of multi-handicapped deaf children aged twelve to fifteen. (November 1984 - April 1985)

John F. Kennedy Memorial Hospital, Hearing and Speech Clinic, Edison, NJ.

Worked with resident Speech Pathologist and Audiologist in screening pre-school children for possible language or hearing difficulties. (June 1984 - August 1984)

PERSONAL

Date of Birth: May 2, 1962; 5'4", 110 lbs.; in excellent health; single.

Energetic, civic minded, avid reader.

Thorough knowledge of sign language and lip reading.

My parents, both of whom are in the teaching profession, have in large measure financed my education, but I contributed a little by babysitting and tutoring when time permitted.

Member of National Student Speech and Hearing Association.

SPEECH AND HEARING THERAPIST (PAGE TWO)

TOM JONES / 100 Main Street, Jamaica, NY 10000 / (100)100-0000

CAREER OBJECTIVE

Holder of New York State teaching certificate wishes to be affiliated with a progressive private school or academy.

EDUCATIONAL BACKGROUND

B.S. degree, Oswego State College, Oswego, NY, June 1987. Major in physical education, minor in sociology. Graduated with 3.75 rating on scale of 4.0.

Extracurricular activities: Captain, varsity swimming team for two consecutive years; Vice President and Executive Secretary, Student Council; Chairman, Social Committee.

CAREER-ORIENTED WORK EXPERIENCE (summer vacations)

Served as assistant to Lou Goldstein, athletic and social director at Grossinger's Resort Hotel, Liberty, NY.

Lifeguard, Jones Beach, NY. State-certified CPR and First Aid techniques.

Athletics Counselor, Eagle's Nest Camp, Bound Brook, NJ. Organized athletic activities for 250 summer campers age 8 to 12. Voted "Outstanding Counselor of the Year" by the Eastern Camp Counselors Association.

PERSONAL

Age 22; height 6'1"; weight 170 lbs; single, no encumbrances. Excellent health; nonsmoker.
Mother, Special Education teacher in local elementary school.
Father, auto mechanic, formerly contender for the middle-weight world boxing championship.
Active in Boy Scouts of America. Selected for National Jamboree and recipient of citation for meritorious service. Currently serve as adult leader.

FUTURE PLANS

To continue studies on a graduate level (evenings and summers) towards a M.S. in Physical Education.

TEACHER

18

LEXICON OF WORDS AND PHRASES FOR RESUMES, COVER LETTERS, AND LETTERS OF APPLICATION

ACTIVE WORDS

Achieved

Accomplished

Accountable for

Activated

Administered

Advanced to position of

Analyzed

Assembled

Assisted

Beat the competition

Broadened

Commended for

Completed

Conducted

Consolidated

Constructed

Contributed

Controlled

Coordinated

Created

Designed

Determined

Developed

Devised

Directed

Established

Evaluated

Expanded

Expedited

Explored

Hands-on experience

Headed

Implemented

Improved

Increased

Initiated

Instituted

Interfaced with

Introduced

Invented

Investigated

Involved with

Launched

Lowered costs

Maintained

Managed

Maximized

Modernized

Monitored

Negotiated

Organized

Originated

Participated in

Perfected

Performed

Pioneered

Planned

Prepared

Produced

Promoted

Published

Recruited

Reduced

Reorganized

Researched

Responsible for

Revised

Revitalized

Set up

Simplified

Spearheaded

Solved

Stabilized

Standardized

Stimulated

Strengthened

Succeeded in

Supervised

Surveyed

Systematized

Targeted

Updated

Upgraded

DESCRIPTIVE WORDS

Able to benefit by constructive
  criticism
Able to learn and teach others
Adaptable
Ambitious
Articulate
Assertive but not pushy
Career-oriented
Civic-minded
Conscientious
Considered attractive
Cooperative
Courteous
Creative
Decisive
Dynamic
Endowed with excellent
  memory
Energetic
Enterprising
Enthusiastic
Even-tempered
Excellent communication
  skills
Expert in the field, but
  not a know- it-all
Flexible
Get along well with people
Happy disposition
Imaginative

Innovative
Intuitive
Leadership ability
Welcome challenge
Like to work, but not a workaholic
Logical
Loyal
Make good appearance
Methodical
Modest, but not humble
Not a clock-watcher
Not a job-hopper
Optimistic
Pace setter
Perceptive
Persevering
Punctual
Reliable
Resourceful
Seasoned professional
Self-motivated
Self-reliant
Self-starter
Stickler for perfection
Superachiever
Tactful
Troubleshooter
Versatile
Well-groomed
Well-organized

19

SCENARIO OF A JOB INTERVIEW

The following scenario is based on the transcript of an interview of a commercial artist responding to an ad placed by a mid-size advertising agency looking for an assistant art director.

Understandably no two interviews are alike. The pattern and procedure followed depend in large measure on the nature of the job applied for, the time allotted to the interview and, often as not, the personality and "style" of the person conducting the interview.

Let's replay the interview proceedings in this instance, from the time the interviewer meets and greets the candidate to the time they go through the formality of shaking hands at the end of the interview.

Interviewer: Sorry for keeping you on hold. The previous candidate showed up 15 minutes later than the time set for the interview, causing the delay.

Candidate: That's okay. I didn't mind waiting. As a matter of fact it gave me an opportunity to see the company citations and awards displayed in the reception room, especially the Graphic Arts Packaging Award, having read about it in a recent issue of *Advertising Age.*

Interviewer: Yes, we're particularly proud of that award since we won it in strong competition with some of the prime advertising agencies in the greater New York area. But let's talk about you. Tell me something about yourself—how you got started, where you got your training, who influenced you most to make art your career, and so forth.

Candidate: I won't bore you with details, but will relate to you with some degree of modesty that at the age of three I already had established a reputation as the best sidewalk artist in the neighborhood. I later advanced to crayolas on paper and whatever I did was highly prized by my grandparents who exhibited my latest creations on the refrigerator doors. So much for that. After graduating from junior high, I was admitted to the High School of Art and Design where I majored in advertising art and lettering. There, with three of my classmates, I organized an art service club, doing the posters and signs for various school activities—dances, student organization election campaigns, athletic meets, and the like. Also, as a member of the newspaper and yearbook staff, I helped with proofreading galleys, selecting photos, and arranging layouts. More than once I skipped lunch to finish up last minute projects to meet printers' deadlines. Oh, I forgot, I didn't neglect my academic studies. As it happened, I won a number of awards—one in creative writing, one in social studies, and twice in a row was on the Dean's List. In addition, I was fortunate enough to have been awarded the Saint-Gaudens Medal for the best art portfolio of the graduating class of 1979. As to who influenced me most to make advertising art my life's career, I shall always be indebted to Ben Clements, Chairman of the Art Department who took a personal interest in me, and by his encouragement bolstered my confidence. On occasion, after school hours, he would invite me to his art service studio to help out with paste-ups, mat cutting, and simple lettering jobs for which I was paid—perhaps more than I was worth.

Interviewer: I note on your resume that you went on to Pratt.

Candidate: Yes, I did. I had been hoping for a scholarship but it didn't come through and so had to finance my own tuition with some help from my parents. You see, the lettering skills I had acquired along the way came in handy. Weekends and after-school hours, I serviced neighborhood stores with display cards, paper signs, and that type of thing, and in time built up quite a clientele. Then, at the end of my sophomore year I was successful in getting a partial scholarship for the next two years. At Pratt, I was an above-average student, entered many contests, won some, and graduated with a B.S. in Advertising Design and Layout.

Interviewer: Tell me how you learned about the job opening here. Do you know anyone in our agency or have you learned through the grapevine that we have an opening for an Assistant Art Director?

Candidate: No to both questions. I came across the ad you placed in *National Employment Business Weekly* and didn't lose any time sending in my resume. I assume that on the strength of it I was invited to appear for an interview, and here I am.

Interviewer: What do you know about our agency and the rank it holds in the advertising field?

Candidate: I've known about the agency for some time, and at the recent Graphic Arts Convention came across your award-winning ads for the Carnegie Hall Concert series. Also, I read about the innovative work done by the agency in the September issue of *Graphic Arts Monthly*. Mr. Larkin, at this point, could you fill me in on the organizational setup of the agency and where I'd fit in?

Interviewer: I am one of the founders of the agency, having formerly been an account executive working for a major art service in my home town, Chicago. We now have a well-coordinated art staff consisting of a senior art director, layout people, several lettering specialists, and a young woman and an assistant handling animation and computer graphics. In addition, we have a number of recent art school graduates doing mechanicals and paste-ups. Ours is a moderate-size organization, and we want to keep it that way. We don't intend to compete in size with McCann-Erickson and other monolithic giants in the business, but give them a run for the money in terms of creativity. If you're hired, you will assist Joan Fuller, our senior art director, with some of the minor accounts, and will be working directly under her supervision.

Candidate: Is this a temporary job for the rush season, or can I assume that it is a permanent staff job?

Interviewer: This happens to be a permanent position. For rush season work and special assignments we use freelancers, as needed. It may interest you to know that in the nine years we've been established, we never had occasion to lay off anyone of our regular staff. We consider each one a member of the family. Incidentally, your resume shows that you've held several short-term jobs before. Can you tell me the reason you left your last job?

Candidate: As a matter of fact, I am still employed there but have decided to make a change. The company I am with has only three other people besides myself in the art department—all of us involved in label design and packaging, catering for the most part to small manufacturers and distributors. As I see it, there are no new challenges, and opportunity for further growth is limited for a person like myself. I feel I'd be wasting my time continuing there indefinitely.

Interviewer: Does your present employer know that you are planning to leave the company?

Candidate: Oh yes, I've discussed it with him, and he agrees that I most likely would do better with a full-service advertising agency where the work will be more diversified and on a higher creative level. He's sorry that I plan to leave and has offered to give me a letter of commendation and highest reference.

Interviewer: I understand what you mean and I want to compliment you for your forthrightness in discussing with your employer your desire to broaden your scope. Would you recommend your present company to any friend or acquaintance?

Candidate: I would do so without hesitation, for anyone starting out on an art career. Work facilities there are somewhat limited but the people are easy to work with. In fact, in discussing with my employer my intention to leave the company, I agreed to help recruit as well as break in my successor within time limitation.

(Interviewer is looking through candidate's portfolio)

Interviewer: Judging by the samples in your portfolio, I see that you are strong in lettering and typographic layout. How well do you handle illustrations?

Candidate: I don't consider myself a professional illustrator. I am able to rough in illustrations as part of a general layout. The samples in the portfolio that have illustrations were rendered by freelance illustrators or photographers under my direction.

Interviewer: A professional opinion: Who would you consider among the foremost type designers who have had the greatest impact on modern advertising typography?

Candidate: I certainly would include people like Benguiat, Lubalin, and Herman Zapf of international fame, and the growing number of younger artists affiliated with the International Typeface Corporation and Photolettering, Inc. In sum, they are the progeny of such classic typographers as Goudy, Bernhard, Trafton, and Middleton.

Interviewer: With so many new developments both technical and creative, how do you keep abreast with what's happening in the advertising field?

Candidate: Well, for one thing, I subscribe to a number of graphic arts publications, principally *Advertising Age, American Artist,* and I get *U&lc,* the avant-garde periodical issued by the International Typeface Corporation. Also, time permitting, I make it a point to attend lectures and seminars sponsored by the American Institute of Graphic Arts, The Art Directors Club of New York, and The Typophiles. I buy the *Art Directors Annual* as soon as it comes off the press and keep old copies for reference.

Interviewer: From the point of view of the creative artist, how will the technical achievements in computer graphics affect the future of our industry?

Candidate: Well, there are those in our profession who are worried that the inroads of the computer will inevitably replace the work of traditional artists. As for me, I look upon computer graphics in its various forms as a tool, not as a bugbear. The fact of the matter is that in the hands of creative people, the scope of the artist will expand immeasurably. This prediction has to a great extent already proven itself, and that's just the beginning.

Interviewer: What, if any, actual experience have you had in the area of computer graphics?

Candidate: Up till now I've had only limited experience. At school, I was one of several students selected for a co-op program, working three afternoons a week for the department of graphics at NBC's Six O'clock News. I was mostly involved with designing spot graphics and credit lines by computer.

Interviewer: Have you had any experience writing or editing advertising copy?

Candidate: Back in my freelance days, when I was designing bookjackets and posters for publishers, I often was asked to write the copy for the blurbs. And also, I occasionally wrote advertising copy for headers for some of the floor display stands I helped to design.

Interviewer: In your present job, did you ever have direct contact with clients of the company?

Candidate: At times I pinch-hit for our salesmen or the boss, making presentations, showing preliminary sketches, comps, and so on, and in other ways acting as liaison between the client and the company.

Interviewer: Looking ahead, do you have a far-reaching goal you would like to talk about?

Candidate: Yes, I'm glad you asked that. My hope is to someday be one of the account executives for this agency. I like the business part of advertising fully as much as working at the drawing board.

Interviewer: That's interesting. We too are looking ahead and are giving some thought to opening a branch in Chicago or on the West Coast. But this is still in the planning stage. If that ever comes about, would you be willing to relocate, perhaps in an administrative or account executive post?

Candidate: I would consider that a new challenge, Mr. Larkin.

Interviewer: To what extent do you require liquor or other stimulants to cope with tension?

Candidate: Personally, I thrive on tension and have no need for any of that to keep in balance.

Interviewer: An offbeat question: It's said that when the late President Anwar Sadat of Egypt was asked what he would like inscribed on his tombstone, he replied that he would like them to say the following: "He lived for peace and died for his principles." Tell me, when the time comes, what would *you* like incribed on *your* tombstone?

Candidate: I may not be able to tell you offhand what inscription might be appropriate for me, but whatever it is, I'd like the wording to be well-spaced and to avoid inscribing the entire epitaph in Old English caps. Answering your question less facetiously, I'd like them to say, "He may not have been right all the time, but was always honest."

Interviewer: On occasion, the work here requires retouching. How good is your vision?

Candidate: Well, when I took my annual eye exam two months ago, I had no difficulty reading the next to the bottom line of the chart without glasses, and I detected slight imperfections in the printing.

Interviewer: What means of transportation would you use to get to work?

Candidate: Though I own a late model Toyota, I wouldn't use it because of occasional traffic snarls and the problems of finding a parking space. I live on East 62nd Street, less than two miles from here, and I'd walk. I need the exercise. When the weather is bad, I can hop on the Second Avenue bus, a couple of blocks away from home. Either way, I'd be sure of getting to work on time, or before.

Interviewer: Would you be able to put in overtime when needed to finish a project, or whatever?

Candidate: I'm used to working late. I burned the midnight oil when I was on my own, freelancing. There'd be no problem on that score—anytime of the week, including weekends. There is only one evening I would not be available for overtime—and that would be on Tuesdays because I give a course on contemporary typography and layouts at Visual Arts. I enjoy the experience and would be disinclined to give it up.

Interviewer: How long have you been a member of the faculty at Visual Arts?

Candidate: I started about two years ago. I am not a regular member of the faculty but serve as an adjunct instructor.

Interviewer: If we hire you, how soon can you start?

Candidate: Well, I would need two weeks after you have given me the green light. I think I owe it to my present employer to help in the orientation of the person who will replace me.

Interviewer: What salary are you looking for?

Candidate: Mr. Larkin, I'll put it to you this way. My present job pays $28,000 a year, in addition to health insurance, bonuses, and perks. I'm looking to start here at five to seven thousand dollars above that figure with periodic increases based on performance on the job, plus the usual benefits package.

Interviewer: Early in the interview you asked whether the position you are applying for is permanent or temporary. I'd like to ask you the same question in a different form. If hired, do you plan to stay on or do you intend to move on to another agency or perhaps enter a new line of business?

Candidate: I plan to stay on this job as long as I can be an asset to the agency and at the same time advance my career goal. I hope I can realize both objectives.

Interviewer: Tell me, do you have any second thoughts about working under the supervision of a female art director?

Candidate: None whatever. Perhaps I'd have to watch my language a bit more carefully, otherwise it wouldn't make any difference. I judge people by their abilities and achievements only, not by their sex, color, religion, or ethnic background.

Interviewer: Are you considering any other job offers at this time?

Candidate: Though I have two tentative offers, for various reasons I would be happiest being associated with your agency.

Interviewer: All things considered, why should we hire you?

Candidate: I feel strongly that I would be an asset to the agency not merely for my professional ability but for my loyalty, background, and my eagerness to grow with the organization. I'm twenty-five years of age, enthusiastic, and optimistic about the future. My mold is not so ironcast as to be inflexible and unwilling to change with the times. I have an impressive record for punctuality and dependability. In short, I believe I'm the man you are looking for. How soon will I know if I have the job?

Interviewer: I can't give you a definite answer until I discuss the matter with Joan Fuller, our senior art director. We most likely will set up another meeting with you within a week or so. All I can say at this time is that you are the frontrunner for the job. Meanwhile, thank you for taking time to come here for the interview. I enjoyed meeting with you.

Candidate: And thank you, Mr. Larkin, for your consideration and courtesy.

NOTE: Three other contenders for the job were dropped after the first interview. This candidate was invited to a subsequent interview and a week later was notified that he was hired for the position at a negotiated salary of $32,500.

Interestingly enough, the decision to offer him the job was based not so much on the extent of work experience (several of the other candidates had as much, if not more hardcore experience) but rather on such intangibles as modesty, tact, spirit of enterprise, enthusiasm, and other desirable personality traits.

20

A PARTING WORD

NOW THAT YOU have diligently gone through the pages of this book once or twice, the difficult task of tracking down a job prospect leading to a successful interview and culminating in an attractive job offer still lies ahead. No book can do more than show the way. The rest is up to you.

I feel certain that the practical information and the many pointers you picked up in this book will, if applied, double your chances not only to be invited to a greater number of interviews, but to come out on top each time, until that special job opportunity you have been looking for materializes. It makes me happy to reflect that I have been in some measure instrumental in bringing this about.

J.I.B.

APPENDICES

• RECOMMENDED READING AND REFERENCES TO OTHER SOURCES

• RESOURCES OF SPECIAL AREAS OF INFORMATION AVAILABLE
THROUGH TRADE AND PROFESSIONAL ASSOCIATIONS

• SAMPLE JOB APPLICATION FORM

• INDEX AND CROSS-REFERENCE

Recommended Reading and References to Other Sources

Books

Azibo, Moni and Therese Crylen Unumb. *The Mature Woman's Back-to-Work Book*. Chicago: Contemporary Books, Inc., 1980.

A helpful guide for women planning to return to the job market. Moni Azibo is coordinator of the CETA Unit of the Displaced Homemaker's Center, Chicago; her collaborator is director of an Illinois County Career Guidance Center. Jointly, they offer practical advice so sorely needed by displaced homemakers who are growing in numbers with each passing year.

Biegeleisen, J.I. *Job Resumes*. New York: Grosset & Dunlap, 1982.

Since the book's first appearance in 1969, it has been acknowledged to be one of the basic books on how to write and present a job resume. It is the only book on resumes suggested by Richard Bolles in his *What Color is Your Parachute?*

Interestingly enough, though Bolles is not one generally inclined to favor resumes as a job-getting tool, he nonetheless refers to it as the historic book in its field.

The book features more than 50 sample resumes, presented in a wide variety of typographic formats covering diverse occupational and professional areas.

Blumenthal, Lassor A. *The Art of Letter Writing*. New York: Putnam Publishing Group, 1986.

The author points out some of the more common grammatical errors and worn-out cliches in spoken and written English, and how to avoid them. The book shows how to compose cover-letters that command attention, thank you letters, letters asking for references—supplemented with appropriate examples. Blumenthal's book serves as a once-over-lightly review of what you may have long forgotten since your school days—or never learned—about letter writing.

Bolles, Richard Nelson. *What Color is Your Parachute?* Berkeley: Ten Speed Press, 1987 (updated periodically).

The title may be a bit obtuse, but the book is a gem! No wonder it has become the most talked about book in its field.

What Color is Your Parachute? is an expression of an outspoken critic and observer in the field of marketing job skills through personal efforts, bypassing expensive (and often inept) counseling firms. The author has the courage to shake up many traditional concepts of job hunting techniques—and he is convincing.

Carnegie, Dale. *How to Win Friends and Influence People*. New York: Simon & Schuster, 1983 edition.

Self-styled sophisticates are apt to look down their noses on Carnegie's book and regard it as an amalgam of platitudes. Ironically enough, these are the very people who need the book most.

There are many professorial-type texts dealing with the principles and psychology of human relations, but what makes this book unique and accounts for the millions of copies sold to date is that it is non-academic in style, very readable, and down-to-earth. The author offers advice that can be applied to practically every phase of human relations. A classic in its field.

Cohen, Herb. *You Can Negotiate Anything*. New York: Bantam Books, 1983.

The book identifies the crucial elements of all negotiation techniques which, according to the author, are the same whether you bargain for a higher starting salary, buy a home, negotiate a contract, or anything else where two or more parties are involved. Practical information on the fine art of negotiation is presented in tongue-in-cheek style by a fluent writer and an acknowledged expert in his field.

Genua, Robert L. *The Employer's Guide to Interviewing*. Englewood Cliffs, NJ: Prentice-Hall, 1979.

It's essential to be aware of how the prospective interviewer assesses the job applicant to see how closely he measures up against a hypothesis of expectations. You'll gain much by thumbing through the pages of this book before you set out for that all-important interview.

Half, Robert. *The Robert Half Way to Get Hired In Today's Job Market*. Chicago: Rawson Wade, 1982.

The author is the founder of a highly rated personnel recruitment network specializing in financial and data processing positions. Reading the book helps the jobseeker in any line of work adjust to the criteria by which he is rated as a prospective employee by the interviewer.

Jackson, Tom. *Guerrilla Tactics in the Job Market*. New York: Bantam Books, 1978.

The author lays forth action-based techniques open to job seekers to broaden their scope of operation through a systematic routine for getting the job they're after. Written in a dynamic style, the message is bound to have a forceable impact on those who follow the author's recommendations.

Mayer, John L. and Donaho, Melvin W. *Get the Right Person for the Right Job*. Englewood Cliffs, NJ: Prentice-Hall, 1979.

Although principally intended as a guide for professional interviewers, this book should prove of value to the interviewee as well. It includes interesting aspects of Affirmative Action and current antidiscriminatory labor laws.

Molloy, John T. *Dress for Success*. New York: Warner Books, 1976.

John Molloy, an acknowledged authority on dress and grooming for business and social occasions, writes about what is embodied in his popular syndicated newspaper column on the subject. His underlying theme is, "You are what you wear." If you dress like a success, you'll feel like one and you'll be regarded as such by others.

Morin, William J. and James C. Cabera. *Parting Company, How to Survive The Loss of a Job, and Find Another Successfully*. New York: Harcourt, Brace, Jovanovich, 1982.

The co-authors show an empathetic understanding of what it means to lose a job. They tell how to make the best use of outplacement counseling services and

other resources to get back on the track, quite often with increased salary and
new career opportunities.

Peale, Norman Vincent. *Positive Imaging*. Old Tappan, NJ: Fleming H. Revell
Co., 1982.

A companion book to the author's *The Power of Positive Thinking*. This is
not a how-to manual but an inspirational book, of value to anyone trying to get
somewhere in the world but lacking the self-image to achieve it. The underlying
message is that what one can imagine, one can be, if reinforced with discipline,
determination, patience, and above all, faith in one's self.

Petras, Ross and Kathryn. *Inside Track: How To Get Into & Succeed in America's Prestige Companies*. New York: Random House, 1986.

Tells about 60 of some of America's most prestigious companies—what it's
like to work for them, what they pay, benefits, perks, chances for advancement,
and how to get a foot in the door.

Instructional Tape Recording

Truitt, John. "How to Get the Highest Salary Offer." Fortson-Truitt Inc., 1981.

This cassette tape is of special interest to those preparing for a job interview and need practical advice on salary negotiation. Side A deals effectively
with the strategy of getting the highest salary offer; side B makes it clear why
proper self-projection is of paramount importance to anyone applying for a job.
The tape is narrated in a concise, down-to-earth fashion by John Truitt,
founder of Executive Search Consultants, a recruitment firm in Houston, Texas.
Though somewhat expensive, it is unquestionably worthwhile having. For particulars, contact: Fortson-Truitt Inc., 4801 Woodway, Suite 300 East, Houston,
TX 77056.

Periodicals Specializing in Employment News and Job Opportunities

Business Week Careers, a monthly journal published by McGraw-Hill Publications.

Includes informative articles on interviewing, resume writing, as well as
many practical tips on job procurement techniques.

Federal Jobs Digest, 325 Pennsylvania Ave SE, Washington, DC 20003.

This bi-weekly, privately published newspaper is devoted exclusively to opportunities in government employment with both civilian and military agencies. Lists current job openings, salaries, requirements.

National Employment Business Weekly, published by Dow Jones & Company, Inc.

This weekly supplement is a veritable treasure trove for career job seekers on the managerial and executive level. Feature articles are contributed by professionals involved in job-search techniques, outplacement organizations, career counselors—all actively engaged in their respective fields. Periodically featured is a classified section listing openings in such diverse fields as electronics, engineering, geothermal physics, computer technology, market research, and sales and management. A Calendar of Events announces workshops, seminars, job clubs, and open-house meetings of special importance to job seekers.

For subscription information, write to National Business Employment Weekly, Dow Jones & Company, Inc., 420 Lexington Ave., New York, NY 10170.

National Job Market, 10406 Muir Place, Kensington, MD 20895.

This bi-weekly newspaper lists private, federal, and overseas career opportunities open to qualified job seekers in many occupations.

Popular Business Magazines

Forbes
Fortune
Barrons
Business Week

Publications such as these, obtainable at newsstands as well as by subscription, will help keep you abreast of current developments and foreseeable prospects in the world of business and industry.

Reference Directories for Researching Business Firms

Standard and Poor's Register of Corporations, Directors and Executives, Standard & Poor's, annual.

This three-volume directory lists more than 37,000 corporations alphabetically, including names, addresses, phone numbers, titles, functions of officers, and principals.

Dun and Bradstreet Million Dollar Directory, Dun & Bradstreet, annual.

Lists firms with a net worth in excess of one million dollars alphabetically, geographically, and by product classification.

Thomas Register of American Manufacturers, Thomas Publishers, annual.

A nationwide advertising directory, alphabetically listing thousands of businesses and services, as well as names and titles of major officers.

Encyclopedia of Associations, Gale Research Co., Detroit, MI.

A compendium of thousands of major trade and professional associations. Brochures and other literature issued by various associations are often available for the asking.

College Placement Annual, College Placement Council, Inc.

This publication is especially useful to recent college graduates preparing to enter the job market. Emphasis is on firms interested in recruiting young college graduates. Listed are specific areas of employment, whom to contact, and addresses.

Directories for Jobs Overseas

Directory of American Firms Operating in Foreign Countries, World Trade Academy Press.

Lists names of approximately 3500 companies operating in foreign countries. It includes names and addresses of persons to contact for overseas jobs.

Trade Lists of American Firms, Subsidiaries and Affiliates

Official directory published by the U.S. Department of Commerce, Washington, DC.

World Trade Directory Reports, published by the U.S. Department of Commerce, Washington, DC.

These reports contain statistics on foreign firms and personnel and may be purchased at nominal cost through any of the field offices of the Department of Commerce.

Foreign Operations, compiled by Foreign Operations, Inc., New Haven, CT.

This publication lists current overseas employment opportunities in American business organizations and U.S. government agencies.

American Register of Exporters, Importers

Lists about 5000 American export and import firms and gives names of key personnel, products handled, and foreign markets.

There is no need to purchase any of these and other specialized directories since they are available in the reference departments of practically all public and business libraries.

*Resources of Specific Areas of Information Available Through Trade
and Professional Associations*

PROFESSIONAL AND SEMI-PROFESSIONAL OCCUPATIONS

ACCOUNTANTS

American Institute of Certified Public
Accountants, 1211 Avenue of the Americas,
New York, NY 10036

American Woman's Society of Certified
Public Accountants, 500 N. Michigan Ave.,
Chicago, IL 60611

AEROSPACE

American Institute of Aeronautics and
Astronautics, 1290 Avenue of the Americas,
New York, NY 10104

ANTHROPOLOGISTS

American Anthropological Association, 1703
New Hampshire Ave., N.W., Washington,
DC 20009

ARCHEOLOGISTS

Archeological Institute of America, 53 Park
Place, New York, NY 10007

ARCHITECTS

American Institute of Architects, 1735 New
York Ave., N.W., Washington, DC 20006

Alliance of Women in Architecture,
P.O. Box 5136, FDR Station, New York,
NY 10022

ARTISTS

Opportunity Resources for the Arts, 1501
Broadway, New York, NY 10016

ASTRONOMERS

American Astronomical Society, 1816
Jefferson Place, N.W., Washington,
DC 20036

BANKERS

American Bankers Association, 1120
Connecticut Ave., N.W., Washington,
DC 20036

BIOCHEMISTS

American Society of Biological Chemists,
9650 Rockeville Pike, Bethesda, MD 20014

BIOLOGISTS

American Institute of Biological Science,
1401 Wilson Blvd., Arlington,
VA 22209

American Society for Cell Biology, 4326
Montgomery Blvd., Bethesda, MD 20014

American Society for Microbiology, 1913 I
St., N.W., Washington, DC 20006

BOTANISTS

American Society for Horticultural Science,
701 N. St. Asoph St., Alexandria, VA 22314

BROADCASTERS

National Association of Broadcasters, 1771 N
St., N.W., Washington, DC 20036

CARTOGRAPHERS

American Congress on Surveying and
Mapping, 210 Little Falls St., Falls Church,
VA 22046

CHEMISTS

American Chemical Society, 1155 16th St.,
N.W., Washington, DC 20036

DATA PROCESSORS

American Federation of Information
Processing Societies, 1815 N. Lynn St.,
Arlington, VA 22209

DENTAL HYGIENISTS

American Dental Hygienists Association, 444 N. Michigan Ave., Chicago, IL 60611

DENTAL LABORATORY ASSISTANTS

American Dental Association, 666 N. Lake Shore Dr., Chicago, IL 60611

DIETICIANS

American Dietetic Association, 430 N. Michigan Ave., Chicago, IL 60611

DRAFTSMEN

American Institute for Design and Drafting, 3119 Price Rd., Bartlesville, OK 74003

ECONOMETRISTS

Institute for Econometric Research, 3471 N. Federal Highway, Ft. Lauderdale, FL 33306

Institute for Mathematical Statistics, Dept. of Statistics and Probability, Michigan State University, East Lansing, MI 48824

ENGINEERS, AGRICULTURAL

American Society of Agricultural Engineers, 2950 Niles Rd., St. Joseph, MI 49085

ENGINEERS, AUDIO

Audio Engineering Society, 60 E. 42nd St., New York, NY 10017

ENGINEERS, AUTOMOTIVE

Society of Automotive Engineers, 400 Commonwealth Drive, Warrendale, PA 15096

ENGINEERS, CHEMICAL

American Inst. of Chemical Engineers, 345 E. 47th St., New York, NY 10017

ENGINEERS, CIVIL

American Society of Civil Engineers, 345 E. 47th St., New York, NY 10017

ENGINEERS, ELECTRICAL

Institute of Electrical and Electronics Engineers, 345 E. 47th St., New York, NY 10017

ENGINEERS, ENVIRONMENTAL

Inter-American Association of Sanitary and Environmental Engineers, 18729 Considine Drive, Brookville, MD 20729

ENGINEERS, HEATING, REFRIGERATING AND AIRCONDITIONING

American Institute of Heating Engineers, 345 E. 47th St., New York, NY 10017

ENGINEERS, INDUSTRIAL

American Institute of Industrial Engineers, 25 Technology Park, Atlanta, Norcross, GA 30092

ENGINEERS, MECHANICAL

American Society of Mechanical Engineers, 345 E. 47th St., New York, NY 10017

ENGINEERS, METALLURGICAL

American Institute of Mining, Metallurgical and Petroleum Engineers, 345 E. 47th St., New York, NY 10017

ENGINEERS, PROFESSIONAL

National Society of Professional Engineers, 2029 K St., N.W., Washington, DC 20006

ENGINEERS, WOMEN

Society of Women Engineers, 345 E. 47th St., New York, NY 10017

FASHION DESIGNERS

Fashion Group, 9 Rockefeller Plaza, New York, NY 10020

FINANCIAL ANALYSTS

New York Society of Security Analysts, 71 Broadway, New York, NY 10006

Financial Analysts Federation, 1633 Broadway, New York, NY 10019

FLIGHT ATTENDANTS

International Flight Attendants Association, P.O. Box 507, Miami Springs, FL 33166

FORESTERS

Society of American Foresters, 5400 Grosvenor Lane, Washington, DC 20014

GEOGRAPHERS

Association of American Geographers, 1710 16th St., N.W., Washington, DC 20009

GEOLOGISTS

American Association of Petroleum Geologists, Box 979, Tulsa, OK 74101

Geological Society of America, 3300 Penrose Place, Boulder, CO 80301

GEOPHYSICISTS

American Geophysical Union, 2000 Florida Ave., Washington, DC 20009

Society of Exploration Geophysicists, Box 3098, Tulsa, OK 74101

HISTORIANS

Organization of American Historians, 112 N. Bryan St., Bloomington, IL 47101

INFORMATION PROCESSORS

American Federation of Information Processing Societies, 1815 N. Lynn St., Arlington, VA 22209

Association for Computing Machinery, 1133 Avenue of the Americas, New York, NY 10036

INTERIOR DESIGNERS AND DECORATORS

American Society of Interior Design, 730 Fifth Ave., New York, NY 10019

JOURNALISTS

American Newspaper Publishers Association, 11600 Sunrise Valley Drive, Reston, VA 22091

LIBRARIANS

American Library Association, 50 East Huron St., Chicago, IL 60611

MATHEMATICIANS

American Mathematical Society, P.O. Box 6248, Providence, RI 02940

Mathematical Association of America, 1529 18th St., N.W., Washington, DC 20036

MEDICAL TECHNOLOGISTS

American Society for Medical Technologists, 330 Meadowfern Drive, Houston, TX 77067

American Medical Technologists, 710 Higgins Road, Park Ridge, IL 60068

METALLURGISTS

American Society for Metals, Metals Park, OH 44073

METEOROLOGISTS

American Meteorology Society, 45 Beacon St., Boston, MA 02108

MICROBIOLOGISTS

American Society for Microbiology, 1913 I St., N.W., Washington, DC 20006

MINEROLOGISTS

Minerological Society of America, 2000 Florida Ave., N.W., Washington, DC 20009

OPTICIANS

Opticians Association of America, 1250 Commonwealth Ave., N.W., Washington, DC 20036

OPTOMETRISTS

American Optometric Association, 243 N. Lindbergh Blvd., St. Louis, MO 63141

NEWSPAPER EDITORS

Associated Press Managing Editors, 50 Rockefeller Plaza, New York, NY 10020

National Federation of Press Women, Box 99, Blue Springs, MS 64015

NURSES

American Nurses Association, 2420 Pershing Road, Kansas City, MO 64108

OCCUPATIONAL THERAPISTS

American Occupational Therapy Association, 1383 Piccard Drive, Rockville, MD 20850

PHARMACISTS

National Association of Retail Druggists, 1750 K St., N.W., Washington, DC 20006

PHOTOGRAPHERS

American Society of Photographers, P.O. Box 1221, 1905 Cornwall Ave., Bellingham, WA 98227

National Press Photographers Association, Box 1146, Durham, NC 27702

PHYSICAL THERAPISTS

American Physical Therapy Association, 1156 15th St., N.W., Washington, DC 20005

PHYSICISTS

American Institute of Physics, 335 E. 45th St., New York, NY 10017

PROGRAMMERS

American Federation of Information Processing Societies, 1815 N. Lynn St., Arlington, VA 22209

PSYCHOLOGISTS

Psychological Society, 100 Beekman St., New York, NY 10038

RADIOLOGY TECHNICIANS

American Society of Radiologic Technologists, 55 E. Jackson Blvd., Chicago, IL 60604

ROBOTIC SPECIALISTS

International Institute for Robotics, Box 210708, Dallas, TX 75211

Robot Institute of America, P.O. Box 930, Dearborn, MI 48128

Robotics International, P.O. Box 930, One SME Drive, Dearborn, MI 48128

SANITARY ENGINEERS

Inter-American Association of Sanitary & Environmental Engineering, 18729 Considine Drive, Brookeville, MD 20729

SECURITY DEALERS

National Association of Security Dealers, 1735 K St., N.W., Washington, DC 20006

SOCIAL WORKERS

National Association of Social Workers, 1425 H St., N.W., Washington, DC 20005

American Geriatric Society, 10 Columbus Circle, New York, NY 10019

SOCIOLOGISTS

American Sociological Association, 1772 N St., N.W., Washington, DC 20036

SYSTEMS ANALYSTS

American Federation of Information Processing Societies, 1815 N. Lynn St., Arlington, VA 22209

TEACHERS

National Education Association, 1201 16th St., N.W., Washington, DC 22036

American Federation of Teachers, 11 Dupont Circle, N.W., Washington, DC 20036

WELDING TECHNOLOGISTS

American Welding Society, 2501 N.W. 7th St., Miami, FL 33125

Welding Institute, P.O. Box 5268, Hilton Head, SC 22928

X-RAY TECHNICIANS

American Society of Radiologic Technologists, 55 E. Jackson Blvd., Chicago, IL 60604

ZOOLOGISTS

American Society of Zoologists, Box 2739, California Lutheran College, Thousands Oaks, CA 91360

ADMINISTRATIVE OCCUPATIONS

ADVERTISING DIRECTORS

American Advertising Federation, 1225 Connecticut Ave., N.W., Washington, DC 20036

National Association for Female Executives, 160 E. 56th St., New York, NY 10022

MANAGEMENT SPECIALISTS

American Management Associations, 135 W. 50th St., New York, NY 10020

National Management Association, 2210 Arbor Blvd., Dayton, OH 45439

PERSONNEL WORKERS

American Personnel & Guidance Association, 5203 Leesburg Pike, Falls Church, VA 22041

International Association of Counseling Services, 2 Skyline Place, Falls Church, VA 22041

International Association for Personnel Women, 150 W. 52nd St., New York, NY 10019

PUBLIC RELATIONS WORKERS

Public Relations Society of America, 845 Third Ave., New York, NY 10022

PURCHASING MANAGERS

National Association of Purchasing Management, 11 Park Place, New York, NY 10007

PERFORMING ARTS OCCUPATIONS

ACTORS

Actors' Equity Association, 165 W. 46th St., New York, NY 10036

Associated Actors and Artists of America, 165 W. 46th St., New York, NY 10036

American Federation of Television and Radio Artists, 1350 Avenue of the Americas, New York, NY 10019

MUSICIANS

American Federation of Musicians of the United States and Canada, 1500 Broadway, New York, NY 10036

SINGERS

National Association of Teachers of Singing, 250 W. 57th St., New York, NY 10107

CLERICAL OCCUPATIONS

OFFICE WORKERS (Secretaries, Stenographers, Typists, Clerks, Bookkeepers, Office Machine Operators)

National Business Education Association, 1914 Association Drive, Reston, VA 22091

American Business Women's Association, 9100 Ward Parkway, Kansas City, MO 64114

National Business League, 4324 Georgia Ave., N.W., Washington, DC 20011

National Secretaries Association, Crown Center, Suite G-10, 2440 Pershing Rd., Kansas City, MO 64108

SALES OCCUPATIONS

INSURANCE AGENTS

Independent Insurance Agents of America, 25 John St., New York, NY 10038

REALTORS

National Association of Realtors, 430 N. Michigan Ave., Chicago, IL 60611

SALESPEOPLE (MANUFACTURERS)

Sales & Marketing Executives International, 380 Lexington Ave., New York, NY 10168

Sales Executive Club of New York, 122 E. 42nd St., New York, NY 10017

SALES REPRESENTATIVES

Bureau of Wholesale Sales Representatives, 1819 Peachtree Road, Atlanta, GA 30309

SALESPEOPLE (RETAIL)

National Retail Merchants Association, 100 W. 31st St., New York, NY 10001

Sales/Manpower Foundation, 122 E. 42nd St., New York, NY 10168

National Council of Salesmen's Organizations, 96 Fulton St., New York, NY 10038

SERVICE OCCUPATIONS

BARBERS

Associated Master Barbers & Beauticians of America, 219 Greenwich Rd., Charlotte, NC 28222

BEAUTICIANS

National Hairdressers and Cosmetologists Association, 3510 Olive St., St. Louis, MO 63103

COSMETOLOGISTS

National Hairdressers & Cosmetologists Association, 3510 Olive St., St. Louis, MO 63103

FBI AGENTS

The Federal Bureau of Investigation, U.S. Department of Justice, Washington, DC 20006

FIREFIGHTERS

International Association of Fire Fighters, 1750 New York Avenue, N.W., Washington, DC 20006

LAW ENFORCEMENT OFFICERS

American Law Enforcement Officers Association, 1100 125th St., N.E., Miami, FL 33161

PRACTICAL NURSES

National Association for Practical Nurse Education and Service, 254 W. 31st St., New York, NY 10001

TRAVEL AGENTS

American Society of Travel Agents, 711
Fifth Avenue, New York, NY 10022

BUILDING TRADE OCCUPATIONS

BRICKLAYERS

International Union of Bricklayers and Allied
Craftsmen, 815 15th St., N.W., Washington,
DC 20005

CARPENTERS

United Brotherhood of Carpenters and Joiners
of America, 101 Constitution Ave., N.W.,
Washington, DC 20001

CEMENT MASONS

International Union of Bricklayers & Allied
Craftsmen, 815 15th St., N.W., Washington,
DC 20005

CONSTRUCTION LABORERS

Laborers International Union of North
America, 905 16th St., N.W., Washington,
DC 20006

ELECTRICIANS

International Brotherhood of Electrical
Workers, 1125 15th St., N.W., Washington,
DC 20005

INSULATING WORKERS

International Association of Heat and Frost
Insulators and Asbestos Workers, 1300
Connecticut Ave., N.W., Washington,
DC 20036

LATHERS

Association of the Wall and Ceiling
Industries International, 1711 Connecticut
Ave., N.W., Washington, DC 20009

MARBLE, TILE SETTERS, AND
TERRAZZO WORKERS

Tile, Marble, Terrazzo Finishers and
Shopmen International Union, 801 N. Putt
St., Alexandria, VA 22314

PAINTERS AND PAPERHANGERS

International Brotherhood of Painters and
Allied Trades, 11750 New York Ave.,
N.W., Washington, DC 20006

PLASTERERS

Operative Plasterers and Cement Masons
International Association of United States and
Canada, 1125 17th St., N.W., Washington,
DC 20036

PLUMBERS AND PIPEFITTERS

United Association of Journeymen and
Apprentices of the Plumbing and Pipefitting
Industry of United States and Canada, 901
Massachusetts Ave., N.W., Washington,
DC 20006

ROOFERS

United Union of Roofers, Waterproofers and
Allied Workers, 1125 17th St., N.W.,
Washington, DC 20036

SHEET METAL WORKERS

Sheet Metal Workers International
Association, 1750 New York Ave., N.W.,
Washington, DC 20006

STONEMASONS

International Union of Bricklayers and Allied
Craftsmen, 815 15th St., N.W., Washington,
DC 20005

STRUCTURAL, ORNAMENTAL, AND
REINFORCING IRON WORKERS

International Association of Bridge, Structural
& Ornamental Iron Workers, 1750 New York
Ave., N.W., Washington, DC 20006

PRINTING OCCUPATIONS

BOOKBINDERS

Graphic Arts International Union, 1900 L St., N.W., Washington, DC 20036

COMPOSING ROOM WORKERS

International Typographic Union, 301 S. Union Blvd. Colorado Springs, CO 80901

Typographers International Association, 2262 Hall Place, Washington, DC 20007

GENERAL

Graphic Arts Technical Foundation, 4615 Forbes Ave., Pittsburgh, PA 15213

International Association of Printing House Craftsmen, 7599 Kenwood Rd., Cincinnati, OH 45236

Screen Printing Association International, 10015 Main St., Fairfax, VA 22031

LITHOGRAPHERS

Printing Industries of America, 1730 N. Lynn St., Arlington, VA 22209

Graphic Arts International Union, 1900 L St., N.W., Washington, DC 20036

PHOTOENGRAVERS

International Association of Photoplatemakers, 552 W. 167th St., South Holland, IL 60473

PRINTING PRESSMEN & ASSISTANTS

International Printing and Graphics Communications Union, 1730 Rhode Island Ave., N.W., Washington, DC 20036

APPLICATION FOR EMPLOYMENT

The Civil Rights Act of 1964 prohibits discrimination in employment because of race, color, religion or national origin.
Public Law 90-202 prohibits discrimination because of age.

PERSONAL INFORMATION

DATE _____ SOCIAL SECURITY NUMBER _____

NAME _____
    LAST   FIRST   MIDDLE

PRESENT ADDRESS _____
    STREET   CITY   STATE

PERMANENT ADDRESS _____
    STREET   CITY   STATE

PHONE No. _____ OWN HOME _____ RENT _____ BOARD _____

IF RELATED TO ANYONE IN OUR EMPLOY, STATE NAME AND DEPARTMENT _____ REFERRED BY _____

EMPLOYMENT DESIRED

POSITION _____ DATE YOU CAN START _____ SALARY DESIRED _____

ARE YOU EMPLOYED NOW? _____ IF SO MAY WE INQUIRE OF YOUR PRESENT EMPLOYER _____

EVER APPLIED TO THIS COMPANY BEFORE? _____ WHERE _____ WHEN _____

EDUCATION	NAME AND LOCATION OF SCHOOL	YEARS ATTENDED	DATE GRADUATED	SUBJECTS STUDIED
GRAMMAR SCHOOL				
HIGH SCHOOL				
COLLEGE				
TRADE, BUSINESS OR CORRESPONDENCE SCHOOL				

SUBJECTS OF SPECIAL STUDY OR RESEARCH WORK _____

_____

WHAT FOREIGN LANGUAGES DO YOU SPEAK FLUENTLY? _____ READ _____ WRITE _____

U.S. MILITARY OR NAVAL SERVICE _____ RANK _____ PRESENT MEMBERSHIP IN NATIONAL GUARD OR RESERVES _____

ACTIVITIES OTHER THAN RELIGIOUS (CIVIC, ATHLETIC, FRATERNAL, ETC.) _____

Seminole Form 5107   (CONTINUED ON OTHER SIDE)

APPLICATION FOR EMPLOYMENT (PAGE ONE)

FORMER EMPLOYERS (LIST BELOW LAST FOUR EMPLOYERS, STARTING WITH LAST ONE FIRST)

DATE MONTH AND YEAR	NAME AND ADDRESS OF EMPLOYER	SALARY	POSITION	REASON FOR LEAVING
FROM _____				
TO _____				
FROM _____				
TO _____				
FROM _____				
TO _____				
FROM _____				
TO _____				

REFERENCES: GIVE BELOW THE NAMES OF THREE PERSONS NOT RELATED TO YOU, WHOM YOU HAVE KNOWN AT LEAST ONE YEAR.

	NAME	ADDRESS	BUSINESS	YEARS ACQUAINTED
1				
2				
3				

PHYSICAL RECORD:
LIST ANY PHYSICAL DEFECTS

WERE YOU EVER INJURED?   GIVE DETAILS

HAVE YOU ANY DEFECTS IN HEARING?   IN VISION?   IN SPEECH?

IN CASE OF
EMERGENCY NOTIFY

               NAME   ADDRESS   PHONE NO.

I AUTHORIZE INVESTIGATION OF ALL STATEMENTS CONTAINED IN THIS APPLICATION. I UNDERSTAND THAT MISREPRESENTATION OR OMISSION OF FACTS CALLED FOR IS CAUSE FOR DISMISSAL. FURTHER, I UNDERSTAND AND AGREE THAT MY EMPLOYMENT IS FOR NO DEFINITE PERIOD AND MAY, REGARDLESS OF THE DATE OF PAYMENT OF MY WAGES AND SALARY, BE TERMINATED AT ANY TIME WITHOUT ANY PREVIOUS NOTICE.

DATE   SIGNATURE

DO NOT WRITE BELOW THIS LINE

INTERVIEWED BY   DATE

REMARKS: _____

NEATNESS		CHARACTER	
PERSONALITY		ABILITY	

HIRED	FOR DEPT:	POSITION	WILL REPORT	SALARY WAGES

APPROVED: 1.   2.   3.
EMPLOYMENT MANAGER   DEPT. HEAD   GENERAL MANAGER

This Application form is made for general use and distribution in the United States and the manufacturer cannot assume responsibility for the inclusion in said form of any questions which may be at variance with local and state laws.

APPLICATION FOR EMPLOYMENT (PAGE TWO)

Index and Cross-Reference